EQUAL TO THE TASK

One Family's Journey
Through Premature Birth

EQUAL TO THE TASK

One Family's Journey
Through Premature Birth

by Dail R. Cantrell

Copyright © 2002 by Dail Cantrell

All rights reserved. No part of this publication may be reproduced, stored in a retrieval system, or transmitted in any form or by any means — electronic, mechanical, photocopy, recording, or any other — except for brief quotations in printed reviews, without the prior permission of the publisher.

Published by InSync Communications LLC, InSync Press
2445 River Tree Circle
Sanford, FL 32771
http://www.insyncpress.com
407-688-1156

This book was set in Adobe Minion
Cover Design and Composition by Jonathan Pennell

Library of Congress Catalog Number:
Cataloging information is available from the Library of Congress.
    Cantrell, Dail R.,
Equal to the Task
    ISBN: 1-929902-16-6

First InSync Press Edition
10 9 8 7 6 5 4 3 2 1
Printed in the United States of America

Any reference to patients/healthcare providers is made with the expressed permission of those named. On any occasion when expressed permission was not given, names and details have been changed to protect the confidentiality of those individuals mentioned.

This publication was designed to provide information in regard to the subject matter covered. In particular, it is designed as a first-person account of a family's experiences in an NICU. It is sold and distributed with the understanding that the publisher and the author are not engaged in rendering medical, legal, or counseling services. If appropriate expert assistance is required, the services of a qualified and competent professional should be sought.

DEDICATION

TO MY MOTHER AND FATHER, Bill and Sarah Cantrell, who have always made me feel that I was special and who taught me about the value of family;

To my grandmother, Ophie Cantrell, who is the only grandparent I ever knew;

To my sister, Ann Cable, who beat me down the path to parenthood and has shown me what I have to look forward to;

And most of all to my wife, Nicki, who is the strongest and most courageous person I have ever known, and to my son Benjamin, because he and his mom showed me what it means to fight.

CONTENTS

Dedication V

Acknowledgment IX

The Author XI

Foreword XII
John Q. Buchheit, M.D. and Stephen C. Prinz, M.D.

Preface XIX

Publisher's Comment XXIII

Free Fall 1

Early Arrival 31

Terror in the Night 47

The Long Way Home...111

Epilogue 217
Nicki Cantrell

Someday I Am Going to Thank You 225

ACKNOWLEDGMENT

GRATEFUL ACKNOWLEDGMENT is made to all of the healthcare providers at the East Tennessee Children's Hospital in Knoxville, Tennessee, for the help they gave me during the writing of this book; and also to my friends, and editors, Carolyn Lea and Kay Davis, without whom this work would not have been possible.

THE AUTHOR

DAIL ROBERT CANTRELL is a lifelong resident of East Tennessee. He received an undergraduate degree from the University of Tennessee and attended graduate school at Lincoln Memorial University before returning to the University of Tennessee to attend law school, where he received the Doctorate of Jurisprudence in 1991.

Dail is the managing partner and senior litigator at Cantrell, Pratt & Varsalona, a position he has held for the past seven years. He is also an adjunct Professor of Law at the University of Tennessee in Knoxville. He is a nationally known trial lawyer and has been active in the ATLA and NACDL. Dail is a recipient of the McClung Medal and the Ray H. Jenkins Award for Excellence in trial advocacy.

Dail and his wife Nicki have been married for five years. They have one son. Although Dail is the author of numerous articles and a textbook, *Equal to the Task* is his first non-legal work.

FOREWORD

A NEONATAL INTENSIVE CARE UNIT (NICU) is a special place within a hospital that is set aside for the care of sick babies. The NICU is staffed by nurses, respiratory therapists, and doctors. All have had training in the care of neonates. The physicians who coordinate the care for these babies are Neonatologists. Neonatologists are pediatric subspecialists who, after completing a pediatrics residency, have done additional fellowship training in the management of critically ill newborns. NICUs have only been a part of American medicine since the mid-1950s. Dr. Stanley James is given credit for establishing the first NICU in the United States at Baby's Hospital at Columbia University Medical Center in New York City. The first NICU in the southeastern United States did not come into existence until one was established by Dr. Billy Andrews at the University of Louisville in 1964. The unit where Benjamin Cantrell was treated was not established until September 1980.

Approximately 10% of all births in the United States are premature. Some of these babies are able to stay in a normal newborn nursery, but many require admission to an NICU. Whether premature or full term, babies are admitted to the NICU when they experience problems with breathing, infection, birth defects, low blood sugar, or low body temperature. Many of them require supplemental oxygen, mechanical ventilation, antibiotics, and intravenous (i.v.) fluids.

They are placed under a radiant warmer or in isolettes to keep them warm while allowing them to use their calories for growth and healing. Frequent lab tests are necessary to monitor the status of their various organ systems. Babies in the NICU are monitored and treated based on the severity of their illness. The sickest newborns require an endotracheal tube placed in their mouth and going into the trachea. This tube is attached to a ventilator which assists the baby with breathing. Before this technology was widely available in the 1970s, many otherwise healthy babies with what would now be considered minor respiratory difficulties were not able to survive. In addition to the tube in their mouth, many babies have i.v. lines in their umbilical cord, scalp, hands, and feet. The babies are also connected by tiny wires to monitors which constantly assess their heart rate, breathing, blood pressure, and blood oxygen levels.

When new parents enter the NICU for the first time, it is overwhelming for them to see their fragile baby connected to so many tubes and wires. In addition, their baby's bed is frequently surrounded by cardiorespiratory monitors, ventilators, i.v. pumps, and a variety of other small machines that are used to sustain the sickest of infants. While the technology is wonderful and many babies would not survive without it, this experience does not generate the warm fuzzy feeling that most people associate with having a new baby.

When they are able to breathe without distress, eat well, maintain their body temperature, and grow, these babies are ready to go home. For some, this is only a few days after their admission to the NICU. For extremely premature babies who may weigh only 1 pound at birth, however, this may mean 3 months or longer in the NICU. In addition to being very expensive, these long NICU stays are emotionally draining for families. As you read Dail Cantrell's account of his son's stay at East Tennessee Children's Hospital, you will get a feeling for some of the ups and downs that Dail and Nicki went through as Benjamin experienced a number of the problems that premature babies born at 32 week's gestation or less encounter.

Time takes on a whole new perspective for parents in the NICU. There is around-the-clock activity, 365 days of the year, at the bedside of these infants. When their baby is having a bad day, it can seem like a week, and a long week can seem like an eternity. Parents whose babies are in the NICU for a month or more frequently report symptoms of burnout. While the primary focus of the NICU staff is taking care of the baby, the family has to be cared for as well. It is crucial to give the family the emotional support that they need as well as the opportunity to voice concerns and to ask questions. Frequently families will open up to a nurse, the NICU social worker, the chaplain, or even parents of other NICU babies with whom they have nothing else in common. These opportunities to discuss their concerns, fears, and hopes are very important for the healing process that parents need to experience. One of the most difficult issues for many parents is the feeling of helplessness that goes with having a critically ill baby. Their normal instinct is to step in and solve all their baby's problems. Unfortunately, this is usually not possible and parents have to rely on the NICU staff to take care of all of their infant's needs. As their baby improves and progresses toward going home, parents are able to recover and to again take control of their lives.

Fortunately, the stress which parents endure and the hard work of the doctors and nurses in the NICU are not in vain because they lead to a good outcome the majority of the time. Over the past 5 years, we have admitted over 2700 babies to our neonatal intensive care unit at East Tennessee Children's Hospital, and more than 97% of them have survived. Some of these survivors continue to face challenges with a variety of medical problems or with their development after discharge. But most of them leave the NICU experience with no long-term sequelae.

In the mid 1970s when several members of our group first started working in neonatology, the overall survival rate for babies admitted to the NICU was only 80 to 85%. In addition, it was rare for a baby under 28 week's gestation to survive and if they did, they almost always had severe complications. Currently, it is not unusual for babies 23 to 24 week's gestation to survive and to have normal development, although there is still room for improvement in this area.

EQUAL TO THE TASK

Just as no two babies are alike, so are no two NICU experiences. The story that follows is a description that is typical for many families who have been through the NICU. We believe it is a story that any family could relate to if they were to ever have a sick child. It is also a story that could help many families anticipate the emotions they might feel while their child is in the NICU and to deal with these emotions more effectively.

Until recently there have been very few books that assist parents in understanding the medical problems and emotional difficulties associated with having a critically ill baby. We recommend without reservation *Equal to the Task* with the hope that it will help families to be more informed and prepare them for the emotional roller coaster they will experience when they have a sick baby in the NICU.

John Q. Buchheit, M.D.
Stephen C. Prinz, M.D.
Knoxville Neonatal Associates, P.C.
East Tennessee Children's Hospital
Knoxville, Tennessee

PUBLISHER'S NOTE: John Quincy Buchheit IV received an M.D. from the University of Tennessee, Memphis, in 1988. He has completed a Residency, Chief Residency, and Fellowship in Pediatrics and Neonatology at the University of Louisville, Kentucky. He is board certified by the American Board of Pediatrics in Neonatal-Perinatal Medicine. Dr. Buchheit is a partner at Knoxville Neonatal Associates, P.C. at East Tennessee Children's Hospital, Knoxville.

Stephen C. Prinz received an M.D. from the University of Tennessee, Memphis, in 1972. He has completed a Residency in Pediatrics at the University of Tennessee Memorial Research Center, Knoxville, and a Fellowship in Neonatal-Perinatal Medicine at the University of Louisville, Kentucky and the University of Kentucky, Lexington. He is board certified by the American Board of Pediatrics in Neonatal-Perinatal Medicine. Dr. Prinz is senior partner at Knoxville Neonatal Associates, P.C. at East Tennessee Children's Hospital, Knoxville.

PREFACE

THIS BOOK HAS A HAPPY ENDING. I feel compelled to say this because the books I read about premature babies during my son's stay in the NICU at East Tennessee Children's Hospital ended in tragedy. I know a writer is not supposed to give away the ending to the book, but I do not want you to be so scared that you do not finish reading this one.

My wife Nicki was admitted to Fort Sanders Regional Medical Center on February 17, 1999. We learned that our unborn son, Benjamin, was experiencing heart failure due to a medical condition called supra ventricular tachycardia (SVT). The doctors did everything they could to treat Nicki, but labor started on February 25 and at 9:50 a.m., Benjamin was born — two and a half months prematurely.

Benjamin was taken from Fort Sanders Regional Medical Center to the East Tennessee Children's Hospital in Knoxville, Tennessee. For the next two and a half months, Benjamin was a patient and Nicki and I, and our parents, were quasi-residents.

During our time in the NICU, I read everything I could find about premature births, which wasn't much. During the long nights when I sat on a stool next to my son's isolette, I asked the doctors and nurses countless questions. I think my habit of taking copious notes was obvious to the nurses because after a couple weeks one of them told me I was taking down so much information that I should write a book. I decided she was right. And now you hold in your hand the finished product.

The fact that you have chosen to pick up this text probably means that you or someone you know has just had a child born prematurely. Or maybe you are an expectant parent who has heard horror stories about what can happen if your child comes early.

The most reassuring statistic that I was given during our stay at the hospital was that over 97% of all premature babies that make it to a NICU ultimately go home. Considering how sick many of these children are, this is an amazing number. But it also says that the odds are that your baby is going to be all right.

In my short time as a father, I have learned that babies are tough. They are a lot more resilient than their moms and dads!

When Benjamin was born, and I became a regular visitor at the NICU, fear was my constant companion. Every time the telephone rang I was afraid that it delivered bad news from the hospital. Every time I entered the nursery and walked back to Benjamin's crib, I was afraid that he had taken a turn for the worse. And I was afraid, perhaps most of all, that I was not man enough to handle a child that was different — a child that was not like the ones that the nurses refer to as "Gerber babies."

I think we fear most what we don't understand. The lack of information, and education, about premature birth is frightening. I remember some of the questions I had:

- How long will Benjamin be in the NICU?
- What do all the machines do?
- What does it mean to go home with a monitor?
- Why are all the signs up about A's and B's?
- Will my baby be normal?
- What is normal?

Nicki and I got through our ordeal because of the interest and attention to detail displayed by our doctors and nurses. Support groups developed naturally among the staff and other parents in the NICU.

Since Benjamin has come home, I have encountered at least twenty people who had babies that spent some time in an NICU. Since all of them asked essentially the same questions, I thought it would be a good idea to share my experiences as a father of a premature baby.

I kept a diary about each day's events. In it are the highs, and lows, that come with any extended hospital stay. I have tried to be as detailed as possible, but still make this book a "good read" — my apologies if the book seems cathartic, but I could not separate what I was feeling from the facts.

If my experiences had to be summarized in one sentence, it would be: "Do not be afraid to hope for miracles." Everyday that Benjamin was in the hospital, my eyes were opened to what life is really all about. The daily struggle offered any number of successes and failures.

I hope you find the information helpful. More importantly, I hope you share it with someone else. Whether you will be in the hospital for a few days, a few weeks, or even months, you will not be able to get through it alone. Part of being a family is "circling the wagons" during times of crisis.

A few years ago, a good friend and his ten-year-old son were killed in a tragic accident. My friend was a minister at a local church. His father, who was also a minister, spoke at the funeral. Through all the tears, I remember the words said by my friend's father as a eulogy: "This too shall pass." I believe that God does not give us any burden that is too great for us to carry. Times of sorrow will be replaced by times of joy. And like every other struggle, "lo' there shall be an ending."

PUBLISHER'S COMMENT

STATISTICALLY, MOST PEOPLE will not find themselves sitting in a hospital waiting room praying for some bit of good news from a physician regarding the status of their newborn son or daughter. For those who have experienced the fear, terror, and indescribable feelings that take over during a time like this, nothing seems to help or ease the mind.

This book is the result of sacrificial love, tremendous anxiety, lots of support, and many seemingly endless days and nights. From the profound depths of near loss, this book emerges as a true testament to one family's steadfast devotion to their child, their love of God, and to the bond between a couple that has grown stronger as the result of a challenge.

Every day in this country, thousands of babies are born. Most of these births are uneventful and proceed without the need for medical intervention. I have often thought that a baby being born without some complication is in itself miraculous. The odds would seem to favor something going wrong. But the opposite is typically true. The little boy in this story, however, was not so lucky. The odds did not go in his favor. And his parents joined the ranks of those who face the challenge of having a premature child.

This is a story that will give any reader chills. It will make you cry. It will make you laugh. You will find it difficult to imagine how any parent could face their worst fears — having to look into the eyes of their only child and wonder: "Why him? Why us?" Perhaps you are just such a parent … or grandparent. An event such as this will touch your life as well as the lives of many around you: relatives, friends, and neighbors … even people who you will never meet, but who hear your story, will be affected.

As you read this story of one family's journey through the events that followed a premature birth, I truly hope that you will also find inspiration and joy. For those of you who now face your own challenges resulting from a premature or threatened birth, my prayers go out to you. Your strength will be tested as never before. The days and perhaps months ahead will surely test even your very soul. But hopefully the story you are about to read will provide you with support and guidance and an increased tenacity that you will be able to pass on to your child.

I know that Dail and Nicki Cantrell send their blessings your way. What they did, you too can do. What their child did, your child can do as well. Strength comes in many different sizes and forms. Perhaps your strength will come from that little one for whom you would give your very life.

Dennis McClellan, *Publisher*

FREE FALL

FEBRUARY 17

HEART FAILURE. Benjamin was dying. Nicki was in the thirtieth week of her pregnancy and our world had just stopped. Benjamin was going to be our first child.

Up until now, Nicki's pregnancy has been textbook. Our appointment today was for a routine checkup that had been scheduled for several weeks. We had no reason to suspect anything was wrong.

Usually we waited for the doctor in one of two brightly decorated rooms that had *Winnie the Pooh* characters wrapped around the feet of the table stirrups. Today, however, we were taken to a tiny corner room with no windows. Other than a couple of charts and an examination table, the room was almost empty. A chair had to be brought in for me so that I would have a place to sit down. In the corner there was an old ultrasound machine, the kind that had levers, like you find on an equalizer.

After a few minutes I became bored and started playing with the controls on the ultrasound. I moved the levers up and down so that they looked like a staircase. Nicki told me to leave them alone, but if I was going to have to wait, I needed something to occupy my time. Besides, we weren't scheduled for an ultrasound.

When Dr. Newton came in she was all business. This was unusual because Dr. Newton doesn't act like a doctor. She is usually warm and relaxed, like a favorite aunt telling you about her latest vacation trip.

Nicki had picked Dr. Newton as her OB because she made pregnancy an event. Dr. Newton is a tiny woman — she can't weigh more than 100 pounds — and her personality is charmingly understated. We never felt rushed, and although she must deal with hundreds of pregnancies each month, we always left with the feeling that our baby was the most important baby in the world.

I knew something was wrong before the doctor said anything. When she listened for Benjamin's heartbeat, it was as if a shadow passed slowly across her face. She hooked Nicki up to the ultrasound. My face must have flushed when Dr. Newton commented that someone had fiddled with the settings, but I was too ashamed to say anything and chose to remain silent. Nicki shot me the "gotcha" glance while stifling a grin. Nicki still didn't suspect that something was wrong.

As soon as Benjamin's image appeared on the screen, Dr. Newton told us that he was in trouble. Fluid had built up in his abdomen. She said this was consistent with "hydrops," a medical term for extra fluid or swelling. It causes heart failure in unborn babies.

I was frozen by her words. Benjamin's heart was beating faster than 250 beats per minute, and it was also irregular. Dr. Newton told us that his condition was life threatening. When she left the room to schedule an emergency appointment with a specialist, Dr. Perry Roussis, Nicki fell into my arms. There was nothing we could do, no one we could to talk to, so we just held on to each other and waited for the doctor to return.

Later, I asked Dr. Newton what she was thinking about when she told us that Benjamin was dying. She said, "I focused on what I could do to help your baby quickly and how I could tell you about this dangerous situation with the least possible alarm." When I asked her why, she replied, "My impression of any pregnancy complication is that the thing moms and dads need most is information."

She was right. I wanted information so desperately that I did not even know how to ask the questions. When Dr. Newton told us that Benjamin could not survive much longer without immediate treatment, I withdrew. My questions were replaced with silence. I was overwhelmed at the thought of losing Benjamin. I felt smothered. I had to force myself to breathe.

I wanted Dr. Newton to say that everything was okay. I wanted to shut my eyes, to close out everything that was happening, to go back to what it was like yesterday — when the only thing I had to worry about was getting the nursery ready.

After a moment, I realized that Dr. Newton wasn't saying anything. When I became aware of the silence, I became even more uneasy. What was I supposed to say? Should I ask questions? Do I want to know? Not knowing leaves room for the lies we tell ourselves when we need something to hold onto. Right now I had nothing.

As I gathered myself, I asked Dr. Newton how she had known that something was wrong. She said that the most important thing she did as a doctor was to listen to her patient. Women develop a "sixth sense" during pregnancy, and when she hears words like "I just don't feel good" or "I'm worried," she and her staff are red flagged that there might be a problem. So when Nurse Gale did the intake part of Nicki's appointment, she heard, or sensed, something when she asked Nicki how she was doing. Because of what Nicki said, the nurse put us in the ultrasound room.

More silence. I didn't want to hear anything else. My stomach felt like someone was squeezing it. I felt like I was on an elevator that was dropping too fast. All I wanted to do was leave. I wanted to go to the specialist right then. I wanted another ultrasound. I wanted Benjamin not to die.

When Dr. Newton said that there was nothing more that could be done until tomorrow, my heart fell. People don't die just between the hours of nine to five. Benjamin needed — I needed —something to be done now. But that's not how it works.

Would Benjamin make it through the night? Why do we have to wait until tomorrow to go to the hospital? Is he going to die? I could not ask these questions either. So an appointment was made with Dr. Roussis for early the next morning. We were told to pack some clothes because Nicki would be admitted to the hospital. The nurse gave Nicki a hug and we walked down the corridor toward the exit from the office. I locked eyes with Dr. Newton as we went past her. With that one look, she answered all of my questions. Benjamin was in trouble and I was about to endure the darkest night of my life.

F E B R U A R Y 1 8

NICKI IS TWENTY-FOUR YEARS OLD. While she was in high school, she found out that she had polycystic kidney fibrosis. This disease causes small tumors to grow in both of her kidneys. The disease is progressive and incurable. The only treatment is a kidney transplant. The disease was passed on to Nicki from her father. There is a fifty/fifty chance that our children will be affected.

Our window of opportunity for having children is small. Nicki's nephrologist has been concerned about how her kidneys would handle the pregnancy. He wanted us to choose an obstetrician who handled high-risk pregnancies. The person he recommended was Dr. Perry Roussis.

Dr. Roussis operates a clinic in Knoxville, Tennessee, next to Fort Sanders Regional Medical Center and East Tennessee Children's Hospital. Nicki and I live about thirty minutes north of Knoxville in Anderson County, Tennessee. Dr. Roussis was one of the obstetricians we interviewed prior to selecting Dr. Newton.

After the interview, Dr. Roussis was quickly crossed off our list. Nicki was unimpressed with his bedside manner. She wanted the process to be fun. I did not look forward to returning to a doctor whom we had rejected.

When we arrived at his clinic that morning, we discovered that our appointment was actually with Dr. Stephens, his partner. Dr. Stephens is a big bear of a man with a gentle voice and kind eyes. Nicki was immediately taken to an examination room and hooked up to one of the several state-of-the-art ultrasound units that are scattered throughout the clinic.

The technician refused to give us any information, which I always think is a bad sign, and told us that the doctor would be in shortly to tell us what was happening. Dr. Stephens soon arrived and told us that Benjamin was experiencing SVT, supra ventricular tachycardia, which was causing his heart to beat at more than twice the normal rate.

Dr. Stephens explained that SVT causes fluid to build up around the lungs. This appears as huge black areas on the ultrasound. To complicate matters, Nicki had gone into labor. This caught us by surprise. Nicki had no idea that she was having contractions. Dr. Stephens told us that if he could not get the labor stopped, Benjamin would die.

Hearing his words took away any hope Nicki and I had created during the night. I had tried to prepare myself for this moment, but I was still clinging to the idea that everything was going be okay — that the specialist would tell us that this was common and could be treated with medicine. I couldn't face the thought of Benjamin dying before I got to hold him.

I just sat there. I don't think he asked us if we had any questions because we were in shock. I felt cold. I couldn't even bring myself to look over at Nicki. I was afraid she would see the panic that was enveloping me like a plastic bag. When the doctor left the room to make arrangements for us to go to the hospital, I wanted to leave, too. For the second time in less than twenty-four hours, I sat next to my wife, alone in an examination room, silently trying to come to terms with losing our baby.

Nicki was going be admitted to Fort Sanders Hospital and taken to one of the delivery rooms. Since the doctor's office is connected to the hospital, Nicki was taken to the hospital in a wheelchair while I went downstairs to fill out the necessary paperwork. I didn't know what to put down when I came to the part that asks for the reason for admittance. I made the mistake of saying that it was for childbirth. The clerk congratulated me and asked if it was a boy or a girl. I mumbled a response, but couldn't bring myself to say that there were complications.

When I finished giving all my insurance information, I set out to find Nicki. The only information I was given was to go to the Second Floor. By the time I located her room, Nicki was already in a bed. Wires had been taped to her stomach, allowing the nurses to record Benjamin's heart rate. This was my first experience with a monitor.

A nurse sat by Nicki's bed making notes as she read from a paper printout that spilled onto the floor. I spent the day watching the monitor. Nicki was given medicine to help her sleep. I was given nothing. I tried to read or occupy myself with television, but I was drawn to the flashing numbers on the screen that registered Benjamin's heart rate. Every time I got the courage to look, I said a silent prayer that it would be in the normal range. Part of me died with every glance.

Monitors are cruel. All they do is confirm what we already know. As the numbers flash, preparing to give a new reading, anticipation builds up and then breaks like the crashing of a wave against a beach. When I look away, I know I am only trying to fool myself into thinking that I don't care what the newest reading will be. I try to resist the urge to watch — but I can't. So every few seconds, I steal a quick glance, like you do when you watch a scary movie through your fingers — afraid to look, but unable to look away.

Nicki was pumped full of medicine and we were told that there was nothing to do but wait and watch. Nurse Karen stayed by Nicki's bedside the entire night, recording the information that came from the machine. When it got really quiet, I could hear the rapid thumping of my son's heart. I imagined that this is a bad dream and if I could just wake up, everything would be OK. But I didn't wake up because this isn't a dream.

So I lay my head back against the chair and I watched. I watched the nurse, I watched Nicki, and I watched the monitor.

I would count seconds until I knew how much time passed between the readings. After a while I could anticipate the change without counting.

The nurse would look from the paper to the screen, making sure that the numbers are the same. They always are. Nothing changes.

The night passed in thirty-second intervals.

F E B R U A R Y 1 9

THIS MORNING DR. ROUSSIS took over Nicki's care. He looks every bit as Greek as his name — jet-black hair, with just a trace of gray around the sides, and a thick dark mustache. I think he looks more like a bandit than a baby doctor. I also think his accent and cosmopolitan manner are intimidating.

The first thing he did was to order another ultrasound. I found it odd that he did it himself rather than reading the results obtained by a technician. Nicki lay back on the table while her mother, Judy, and I watched over his shoulder. A large screen was suspended from the ceiling so that we could see the outline of Benjamin's body lying completely still in a sea of black.

Dr. Roussis poked Nicki on the stomach trying to get Benjamin to move. When he just lay there, I wanted to scream, to cry out. I wanted some sign that he was not dead — but there was nothing. Dr. Roussis flicked his fingers against Nicki's abdomen trying to get a reaction. A small spontaneous movement of Benjamin's arm was all that happened.

As Nicki was having the gel cleaned off, we got the diagnosis. If Nicki delivered, Benjamin would be stillborn. His only chance was if the doctors could get his heart to convert, which I assumed must mean to slow down.

For the next several hours I would sit in a chair next to Nicki's bed and lay my head against her stomach trying to feel Benjamin move, searching for anything to cling to. And I would lie to her, and to myself, saying that I felt something. But there was nothing — no movement, no hope.

Neither one of us has cried today. Although we didn't say it, I think that we are afraid that crying means giving up. We have been in a freefall for three days.

Later in the afternoon, Dr. Roussis tried to talk to us about what was happening, but we were all out of words. He must have sensed our mood because he got up from his stool and went into the hallway. He returned with a portable ultrasound machine. There were no nurses, no technicians, just the three of us.

Without saying anything, he squirted the gel onto Nicki's belly and showed us Benjamin. Then he caught our eyes, took Nicki by the hand, and said, "This is why you are fighting."

For the next twenty minutes, the three of us sat there and watched the monitor. No one interrupted us. Nothing was said. We just looked at our son. Finally Dr. Roussis stood up, kissed Nicki on the head, winked at me, and said, "Get some sleep, you'll need it."

It wasn't what he said, but how he said it — no panic or sense of urgency. He even grinned. It was the first moment since all of this started that I honestly believed that Benjamin would not die. I was completely caught up in his confidence. Benjamin was going to live. Dr. Rousis knew it and he brought Nicki and me along with him.

For the past couple of days I had tried to prepare myself for Benjamin's death: I would be strong for Nicki. We would have other children. We would get past this. I had been afraid to even hope that he would live. I do not think I can survive having this tiny bit of hope taken from me, but Dr. Roussis was not ready to give up and neither should we.

That night the medicine made Nicki sleep. I sat over in the corner and watched her. Except for the nurse that sat by her bedside recording the data coming from the monitor, we were alone. Nicki's head had rolled to one side, facing toward where I sat. Her breathing was slow and labored. Her eyes were shut, but the look on her face was tense — her jaw looked like it was clenched.

I wondered what she was dreaming about. I hope they are good dreams. I wonder how it is possible for her to sleep with all that is happening.

The nurse is quiet. She doesn't talk or move around. She has turned all of the lights off and is working from the faint glow of the monitors. My eyes have become accustomed to the dark, so I can see everything clearly. I am beginning to think that it never gets completely dark in a hospital.

The machines that are hooked up to Nicki make me remember when my father had a heart attack and needed an emergency bypass. The doctors told us that there was a significant risk that he would not make it through the surgery so they let us in to see him one by one. Pop had tubes everywhere. Although he could not speak, he looked me in the eye, raised his left hand, and made a fist. He would not die. He was a fighter.

What Dr. Roussis gave Nicki today was not hope, but an opportunity — an opportunity that was worth the struggle that lay before her. If he believed, so could she. As Nicki lay sleeping, resting for what was to come, I knew that her child would not be taken from her without a fight.

Nicki may be scared, but she is not afraid to fight.

FREE FALL

FEBRUARY 20

EARLY THIS MORNING, Dr. Roussis began injecting magnesium into Nicki's i.v. He told her that tomorrow she would hate him, but the day after that she would love him. The magnesium was to stop the contractions. Benjamin's life depended on Nicki's ability to prevent delivery. This would allow his heart to convert so that the fluid would clear from his chest. She was also given steroids to help his lungs develop.

Nicki was kept in a delivery room. These rooms don't have even the basic comforts that come with a standard hospital room because the occupant is not expected to be there for more than a few hours. The temperature was kept between 60 and 65 degrees. There was no carpet on the floor, no pictures on the wall, just a bed, lots of machines, and several locked cabinets.

Every few hours, Dr. Roussis did another ultrasound to see if there was any progress. There wasn't. I can't get my hopes up anymore.

That afternoon Nicki's dad, Jack, came to the hospital. When he received word that Nicki was in trouble, he drove from out of state to see her. The two of them embraced. They didn't need to talk. Hugs were enough.

Nicki is in her second year of law school. We had planned Benjamin's birth around her classes. She is an honor student and a member of the Phi Beta Kappa society for academic excellence. It is hard on her to not be in control of what was happening.

As she talked to her father, she told him about what was being done. Never once did she mention that Benjamin might die. I wish I had her confidence — her faith. The only thing I can think about is Benjamin dying. With every ultrasound, I prepare myself for the sight of him lying dead in Nicki's stomach. Every time the doctor comes in, I brace myself. I feel like I am dying.

As I listen to Nicki and Jack, they talk as if nothing is wrong. Why can't she see the truth? She is in denial. Thinking about it made me so angry I had to leave the room. I walked outside and stood next to the entrance to the emergency room. It was cold. I had no jacket — nothing but my cap and a sweatshirt.

Why can't Nicki accept the fact that Benjamin is going to die? I refuse to cover myself with false hope. He's not going to get any better, so we should be preparing ourselves.

It began to rain and I moved inside. I found a seat in the corner of the emergency room waiting area. No one sat near me.

I began to talk to God — silently — with my eyes open. I didn't ask for anything —I just talked.

I want to believe.

~~~ FREE FALL ~~~

FEBRUARY 21

DR. ROUSSIS WAS RIGHT. Today Nicki hated him. The magnesium made her sick. I don't mean sick like when you become nauseous, but the type of sick that crawls all over you. She couldn't eat. She couldn't get comfortable. She couldn't even escape with sleep.

Dr. Roussis came by at lunchtime and gave us the "sit-down" talk. Doctors give you information in stages because they realize that when you first hear bad news, your mind immediately goes into shutdown. They explain the clinical data necessary for you to make decisions only after you have recovered from the initial shock. I call it the warm towel theory. You don't really appreciate a warm towel until after you've taken a cold shower. The bad news was our cold shower and the clinical information would be our warm towel — for now.

Dr. Roussis drew a diagram of the heart. One of Benjamin's valves was not shutting which was causing his heart to beat at twice its normal speed. Nicki was acting as his life support system. The medicine being pumped into her, and therefore into Benjamin, was to slow his heart, allowing the valve to close so the fluid could dissipate.

If Benjamin were delivered now, he would lose his life support system and the doctors would have to do artificially what Nicki was doing naturally. This would be bad and Benjamin's chance of survival would be almost zero. Dr. Roussis felt the best plan of treatment was to stop Nicki's labor and allow Benjamin's heart to convert while he was still in the womb. The big question was whether or not Nicki would be strong enough to hold out.

Her body was under constant stress. She was having difficulty breathing, and the medicine that the doctors were giving Benjamin to slow his heart was having the same effect on Nicki. The doctors were also concerned about how the magnesium treatment was affecting Nicki's kidney function. Her blood pressure was high — at one point she went into respiratory failure. A cardiologist was brought in to monitor Nicki while Dr. Roussis took care of Benjamin.

A problem pregnancy — the threat of a premature birth — is difficult enough without the psychological torture of knowing that if you allow your body to do what it wants to do, which is to deliver, you are guaranteeing the death of the life you carry. Nicki was tiring.

That afternoon, Steve, a friend who is a massage therapist, came by the hospital and worked on Nicki for almost two hours. Any expectant father who wants to earn a lifetime worth of Brownie points needs to have a masseuse come to the delivery room.

FREE FALL

I had never seen anyone get a massage before, so I sat behind Steve while he worked on Nicki. Delivery beds are not designed for anyone to lie on them except for more than a few hours. The bed was causing the muscles in her back to spasm. Steve took small dollops of lotion and placed them on various muscle groups. I watched as he worked on the different pressure points. Her muscles relaxed and spread out.

When he was finished, the nurses came in and took Nicki for a shower. We had been in the hospital for four days and she had not been allowed to bathe. There are no showers in any of the delivery rooms. Arrangements were made to take Nicki to the doctor's lounge. The nurses helped her undress and sat her on a chair. They even got into the shower with her. It was like watching a trainer work on a boxer between rounds.

Although we have been married for two years, I did not know that my wife was a warrior. Once Dr. Roussis gave her a job to do, she decided it would be done even if it meant dying herself. She would not allow her body to relax. If Dr. Roussis believed, then so would she.

Today, however, she still hated him.

FEBRUARY 22

AT 3:00 A.M. Benjamin's heart converted! I was wide-awake when it happened. This was not surprising because I have been awake for twenty-three of the last twenty-four hours. Watching the monitors and coping with all the stress made sleep impossible.

My bed has been a chair that unfolds into a cot. It's like sleeping on a stack of two-by-fours. I can only assume that the hospital is trying to help me share in the birthing process by making me as uncomfortable as possible.

Nicki was moved to the Sixth Floor late in the afternoon. This is where all of the expectant mothers stay, and it is the first room that newborn babies call home. When this happened, I experienced a "moment of enlightenment."

I am thirty-four years old and I have had few epiphanies. These moments occur when one of life's truths is revealed. My first came while I was an undergraduate at the University of Tennessee. I was in a large lecture hall when for some reason it dawned on me what the expression "Damn the torpedoes, full speed ahead!" meant.

I can't remember when I first heard this phrase. It is one of those things that you just know without really knowing how you know it. I probably heard it on television or in a movie because that is where you hear such things. Until that morning, when I was being put to sleep by a droning professor in a freshman astronomy class, I never knew what that saying meant.

It's not the words that have meaning, but the spirit in which they are said that matters. You have to be faced with a no-win situation, with time running out, and nothing left to lose. You can quit, and accept defeat, or you can go into battle — "Damn the torpedoes, full speed ahead."

The comma between "torpedoes" and "full" that is read, but rarely spoken, makes all of the difference. "Understanding" can be separated from "knowing" by something as simple as a comma. Read the phrase, as it relates to the story being told, and the meaning is clear. Taken out of context, the spoken words mean nothing. They have to be seen, not heard.

This was my first step toward adulthood. It was like waking from a long sleep and being able to see something for the first time. No matter how many times someone describes the color blue, you can't really appreciate it unless you see it for yourself. When Nicki was moved to the Sixth Floor, I experienced another such moment. It occurred when we received our first bouquet of flowers.

I have always hated flowers. We don't keep plants at our house and I don't allow flowers at the office. I don't even like the smell of flowers. For funerals, I was always a "book man."

When Nicki and I got the first vase filled with flowers, we put them in the window of her hospital room. They made us feel better almost immediately. Every time another arrangement came, our spirits were lifted even more.

I never thought that getting flowers would make such a difference. I guess it's because I never thought about flowers in the right context. I had always looked at sending flowers as a big waste. Today, in that hospital room with Nicki fighting for Benjamin's life, the flowers meant so much more.

The flowers gave us strength. Each arrangement had message from a friend or family — a word of encouragement or comfort.

As the flowers came, they began to fill the room. Each new vase required that I rearrange our "garden," under Nicki's direction, so that she could see every flower.

They were all beautiful. Every note was carefully read, and saved, as a reminder of the love that they represented. It meant so much to see the room filled with flowers because it was a visual statement of how many people were thinking about us.

By nighttime, there was no place left to put the vases. Space was made for the bigger arrangements on the floor. The room was filled with the aroma of a hundred different smells. It made everything seem less sterile. The flowers brought us peace. "Damn the torpedoes, full speed ahead!"

Dr. Roussis was right — today Nicki loved him.

FREE FALL

FEBRUARY 23

S TAYING IN A HOSPITAL is a lot like going to school. You fall into a routine and draw comfort by being able to follow a schedule. Nicki and I know what time the tests occur and when the doctors will come by.

I don't go to work and I only leave Nicki long enough to go get food. Although we have only been in the hospital for a week, we have adapted our lives to fit a schedule that has been thrust upon us. I am living in a world that I could not even have imagined a week ago.

My partner, Bill Pratt, told me that you don't start living until you experience failure. He believes that you have to get up from being knocked down before you can see life for what it really is — a series of episodes separated by tragedy and success.

The first failure that I remember occurred in college during my first semester. The class I was taking was Basic Engineering. I had never been a great student, but my grades were always solid. I was one of about three hundred freshmen in the class and I felt that I could make a B with minimal effort.

After the first exam, the professor posted the grades on the bulletin board. The high was a 98 and the low was a 40. The class average was 67. He then proceeded to call out names, going from the highest to the lowest grade. I was sitting on the back row of the huge lecture hall and I could see what the people around me were getting. I watched as my fellow students returned to their seats with grades that ranged from the 90s to the 80s. I felt I had made a low 80 — perhaps a high 70. I didn't become concerned until the girl in front of me got a 68.

As the professor continued to call out the names, I saw the grades drop from the 60s to the 50s. When I saw a 49, I knew that there must be a mistake — he had missed my test. After about twenty minutes, the professor paused and said, "And finally, Mr. Cantrell." I was stunned. I had to walk down from the back of the room to get my paper. As I returned to my seat, I caught my classmates looking at me. I knew what they were thinking — "At least I beat Mr. Cantrell."

Real failure is the kind you can't hide from. It can't remain a secret. People have to see you fail so that you will be accountable.

Pratt is right. You have to fail, in public, to see how you will be measured as a person.

These last few days have been hard. I can't help but feel that somehow I am failing as a father. I feel like I'm dreaming the dream where I am naked, trying to hide.

Everyone knows I'm scared. I can do nothing to help Nicki. I just sit all day, trying to hide, so I won't have to answer questions or look at myself.

FREE FALL

I have fallen. I've been broken. And I don't know if I will struggle back up. Or even if I can.

F E B R U A R Y 2 4

TEAM CANTRELL HAD A MEETING with both Dr. Stephens and Dr. Roussis this morning. Benjamin is moving out of danger. The monitors were unhooked so Nicki could get out of bed and walk around. The doctors want to delay the birth for another two weeks, but if Benjamin has to come sooner, he would live. I felt like I was coming out of a long tunnel. That afternoon I left the hospital for the first time in almost a week. I had to teach a class at the law school.

I have been an attorney for almost ten years. For the last five I have also worked as an adjunct professor for the University of Tennessee. I teach in the advocacy department of the law school. My class meets once a week for three hours. I teach trial practice — the nuts and bolts of a trial. Tonight was my first class since Benjamin had gotten sick.

The students are wonderful. I learn more from them than I teach. It was refreshing to get out of the hospital for a while.

When I returned, Judy met me at the doorway. She said the doctors wanted to speak with me, but they wanted to do it out of Nicki's presence. That scared me.

It was a little after eight in the evening. The two of them were waiting for me at the nurses' station. We walked over to a corner in the hallway and Dr. Stephens tentatively told me that my insurance company did not want to pay for Nicki's continued stay in the hospital.

The doctors felt that Nicki needed to remain hospitalized and they were tiptoeing around asking me to assist them in putting some pressure on the insurance company. I work with insurance companies on a daily basis and the commercials that imply that they are "like a good neighbor" are a pile of hooey. The only thing that the "good hands" people care about is giving you a "piece of the rock."

In short order, I told the doctors that they need not concern themselves with my insurance company — that the next morning I would personally contact the claims handler, who had never met my wife, and inform him that I would have a bad-faith lawsuit served before lunch. In perfect unison, both of them grinned.

After I met with the doctors, Judy said a quick goodnight. Nicki and I had our best evening yet. We watched two of my favorite shows, *American Justice* and *Law and Order*, and took a long walk around the floor, taking time to look at the new babies. We even began to laugh about our experience. I decided that I would go to work in the morning. My plans changed when Nicki's water broke at 5 a.m.

# FREE FALL

FEBRUARY 25

I HAD JUST MANAGED to doze off when Nicki called out to me from the bathroom. I went to her and she started crying. She said that her water had broken and told me to go get a nurse.

Nicki has been a gladiator. Although she has been in labor for more than a week, she was determined that our child would live. She suffered through the medicines, the tests, and the uncertainty, without ever losing sight of the goal. No quarter was asked — none was given.

I have been a coach for almost all of my adult life. I coach volleyball and basketball at Anderson County High School. The hardest thing to teach an athlete is that there is no shame in losing when you have given your best. Championships go to only a select few, but that does not mean that the others who ran the race or played the game have failed. I tried to tell Nicki that we were here, and Benjamin had his chance, because of her. She was inconsolable.

As Nicki was taken back downstairs to the delivery room, I was given the responsibility of calling the appropriate family members. Nicki was given an injection of a drug called Stadol and she began a long ride on the mood swing roller coaster. She went from chatty giddiness to unrelenting anger caused by the release of pent-up frustration. In no uncertain terms, Nicki told her mother and me that it was time for the epidural.

I do not know how a starving animal would react if you tried to pull food from its mouth, but it cannot be any less fierce than a pregnant woman about to give birth who wants pain medication. Judy and I tried to convince Nicki that we were not part of a vast conspiracy to keep the pain medicine from her.

By 8:00 that morning, everyone had arrived, meaning all of the grandparents, my sister, and our close friends. At 8:30 we were told that we should expect Benjamin's arrival to be between 12:00 and 1:00. I was exhausted. I tried to grab a quick nap so that I would have the energy to get through the birth.

I had just closed my eyes when Nicki told me she was feeling some pressure. At that moment everything exploded. Dr. Roussis came into the room and scrubbed as he yelled out instructions to the nurses who were putting up lights and pulling machines from locked cabinets that I had never seen opened. One of them made a call to Children's Hospital to have a neonatologist present. I experienced my first birth.

Growing up, I never had a cat, so I never saw kittens being born. For that matter, I have never seen anything born. Whenever a birth occurred on television, I either left the room or changed the channel. I don't even like to talk about female hygiene. I would prefer to remain ignorant about the entire process. To say that I was reluctant to be a participant in Benjamin's birth would be an understatement.

I couldn't bring myself to look beyond the sheet. In fact, I passed out. I was holding Nicki's hand and the next thing I remember was waking up as a nurse placed a cold compress on the back of my neck. I spent the next few minutes with my eyes staring at the floor, holding Nicki's hand telling her that she was doing great.

Nicki had given me a book to read which detailed everything that occurred during childbirth. I meant to read it, but had kept putting it off. I thought I had more time. With everything that was happening, I felt like a rabbit caught in the headlights of a speeding truck. Like the rabbits in *Watership Down*, I went "tharn." Why didn't I read that stupid book!

Dr. Roussis kept me involved with stories about Greece and the fact that Nicki stood for victory and was where the word "Nike" came from. The highlight was when he told me that he had delivered Rick Pitino's baby. For the average person, this might not mean anything, but to me the Boston Celtics are almost synonymous with religion. I have seats from the Boston Garden in my office and autographed pictures from every Celtic since Cousey. I did not think that this man could rise any higher in stature until he mentioned that he had been entrusted with the birth of baby Pitino.

It is impossible to put into words what goes on in a delivery room. I would be lying if I said I enjoyed it or that I recommended it. The event is overwhelming.

At 9:50 that morning Benjamin was born. As soon as Dr. Roussis pulled him out, he held him up for us to see. Nicki was not wearing her glasses and as her mother reached across the table, she knocked them onto the floor. This elicited a curse word from Judy. That was probably the first thing that Benjamin heard.

Dr. Roussis handed Benjamin over to Dr. Nalle, the neonatologist, who had brought an isolette with him from Children's Hospital. Before Benjamin was taken to Children's Hospital, Nicki and I were allowed to put our hands through the openings in the glass and touch our son for the first time. He is beautiful.

One of the nurses had a Polaroid™ camera and began shooting pictures. I put my index finger through the opening into his bed. He grabbed hold of it. His eyes were not open, and I don't even know if he knew that I was his father, but for the first time in my life I touched someone who is part of me.

When I was an infant, Mom and Pop adopted me. Mom used to tell me that I was more special than any other baby in the world because she and Pop got to pick me out while all of the other parents had to take what they got. I could not have had better parents. Although I rarely think about being adopted, when my sister Ann's son was born, it left me with an odd feeling. Ann was also adopted and seeing someone that looked like her made me feel empty.

My Mom and Pop were the perfect parents, and I would not trade them for any others. The people who gave birth to me have no place in my life. I have no desire to ever meet them or to know anything about them. The only parents that I have, or that I will ever have, are Bill and Sarah Cantrell. Still, touching Benjamin's hand was magical.

As the oxygen in the isolette began to run low, Benjamin was taken over to Children's Hospital with the friends and grandparents in tow. This left Nicki and me alone for the first time in more than a week. I crawled up onto the bed with her and we held each other, laughing and praying.

That night I refused to go see Benjamin until Nicki could come with me. It was then that we got our first long look. Benjamin is in a little plastic oxygen hood. It looks like a cake plate to me. It sits over his head. Other than that, he is perfect. All of the grandparents got to come in, and Kay and George, longtime friends, slipped in under the pretext of being grandparents. They were the first non-family members to see Benjamin. They took his picture to put on the Internet.

Everything that happened during the past week was forgotten. Benjamin is alive. So am I.

Standing by his crib, actually seeing him in the flesh, not his outline, is like looking at a sunrise. I feel like I can start to live again. I want to cry and laugh at the same time. It is what I had imagined it was supposed to be like, only better.

We couldn't hold him yet. That would come later. His heart is beating like a baby's heart is supposed to beat. He is still and his eyes are closed, but I could see him breathe.

The nurse said that we shouldn't touch him — too much. We held his leg and his hand. His little face is red and scrunched up. His hair is dark like Nicki's.

His fingers are so small, but his hands are huge. They look like gloves. He could palm a tennis ball.

Benjamin is now my son. He always was mine, but it's different when he's in a crib instead of inside Nicki. This is the greatest day of my life. It's cliché to say, but it's true.

I went to bed that night and actually slept.

EARLY ARRIVAL

FEBRUARY 26

NICKI SLEPT MOST OF THE MORNING so we did not visit Benjamin until late this afternoon. Logistically we are having some problems. Nicki is still a patient at Fort Sanders Regional Medical Center while Benjamin is across the street in the Neonatal Intensive Care Unit (NICU) at Children's Hospital.

Since Nicki is still a patient, she is not allowed to leave the hospital unescorted. To get to Children's Hospital, we had to make arrangements with an orderly to take us down a service elevator, past the cafeteria, to a tunnel that is underneath the street. The tunnel is brightly decorated with cartoon characters and it is at a forty-five degree downhill grade.

The angle of the floor made travel difficult because Nicki is in a wheelchair. The orderly had to struggle to hold on to it. I did a skip step to keep up with them, all the while wondering how we were going to push her up that steep grade when we came back.

It is about 150 yards through the tunnel to an elevator in the basement of Children's Hospital. The NICU is on the Fifth Floor. This is where newborn babies who have health problems ranging from premature birth to serious birth defects are taken.

Security at the NICU is tight. To get inside the nursery, a set procedure has to be followed. First, you to go an intercom and identify yourself. Then you hear a buzzer when the door is unlocked. Only parents and grandparents are allowed inside. Next, you are taken to the scrub-in room. This room is really more like a hallway than a room. It's about eight feet long and three feet wide. Two large sinks with disinfectant soap and scrub brushes sit between stacks of gowns and masks. Visitors are required to scrub, up to their elbows, for no less than 5 minutes. Then you dress in a surgical gown. The masks are optional.

On the wall across from the sinks is a bulletin board with information about infant CPR classes, various charts, and schedules. Only two people are allowed in the scrub-in area at a time. I don't think any more than that could fit in there anyway. When you finish scrubbing in, the next set of parents is buzzed in as you pass into the next room.

After you scrub-in, you go to a secondary waiting area. This is where you receive any special instructions. It is also where the head nurse stays. A large X-ray viewing machine is on one wall. The rest of the room is full of charts and records. The person pushing the buzzer to let you in keeps a record of everyone that comes and goes from the room. This is for security.

Next to the records area is a small workstation for the doctors. Other than the chairs used by the staff, there are no other places to sit. The room is shaped like an "S" and can't be seen from the outside. It is obvious that this is a high-traffic area. It has not been designed for standing or talking. It merely separates the scrub-in area from the nursery and allows the doctors and nurses to have a central area for record keeping.

The nursery is a large room that is about sixty feet long by twenty feet wide. It has three entrances/exits. Parents and staff enter from the security checkpoint door outside of the scrub-in area. The doorway in the middle of the room is used to bring in new babies. Across from the parents' entrance is a fire exit door.

An observation window separates the nursery from the outside waiting area. As you come off the elevator, the window is straight in front of you. It is a large window, probably five feet by four feet. All of the critical care beds can be seen from this window. Friends and family crowd around it trying to see their baby.

There are no walls in the NICU. Short dividers separate the room into three sections. The first row of dividers divides the room into two long halves. About two thirds of the way toward the back of the room, a hallway-type area forms a small section in the back of the room which contains four cribs and an isolation room.

There are thirty-six cribs. Twelve of these cribs are critical care units, reserved for babies with the most serious problems and for the new arrivals. This area is called Stage I and it is located in the left corner of the room. The cribs are arranged six to a side with a small aisle between them.

"Crib" is not a good word to describe these units. All twelve of the critical care spaces are fully equipped with every possible monitor and machine. Several of the babies have been intubated and require oxygen, while others, like Benjamin, are just being monitored for health concerns such as heart irregularities or bowel disease. Typically one nurse is assigned to each critical baby, with the less critical ones sharing a nurse.

The entire section is designed to be open so the doctors and nurses have room to work if there is an emergency. The room is well lighted. The floor is gray with hospital-type tile. The walls are off-white. The only decoration is a simple wallpaper border around the top of the walls — a nursery pattern with bears. Several wooden rocking chairs are scattered throughout the nursery. There are also tall metal stools with short backs pulled up beside the cribs.

There is a nurse's station that separates Stage I from Stage II. Stage II is for babies who are no longer critical, but who still require extra attention. There is a large isolation room in this section in case a baby needs special care.

At the end of the room, which can't be seen from the viewing window, is Stage III. This is for the feeder-growers. These babies are just waiting to get strong enough to go home. Babies have to weigh at least four pounds and be able to eat before they can leave the NICU.

Each crib has a large tray of supplies located at the foot. The top of the tray is flat. The baby's chart is kept on this tray in a three-ring notebook which is updated daily. The chart is for the nurses, doctors, and parents.

EARLY ARRIVAL

There are five neonatologists who serve as staff in the NICU: Dr. Prinz, Dr. Wooldridge, Dr. Nalle, Dr. Howick, and Dr. Buchheit. At least one doctor is in the nursery at all times — twenty-four hours a day, seven days a week

One doctor is assigned to Stage I and another one is assigned to Stages II and III. The doctor for each stage is the primary doctor for an entire month. This allows for continuity of care. The other three doctors provide back-up for the two primary physicians. At the end of each month, they rotate.

The nurses work twelve-hour shifts. Based on experience and ability, they are assigned to the babies who need the most care. There are visiting hours from 8:30 a.m. until 6:00 p.m. and from 8:30 p.m. until 6:00 a.m. No visitors are allowed between 6:00 and 8:30 both morning and evening so the doctors and nurses can prepare for shift change.

There are only a few rules at the NICU, but these rules are strictly enforced. Rule Number One is that only parents and grandparents are allowed to go into the nursery to see the baby. Rule Number Two is that only two individuals are allowed at one time. And Rule Number Three is that you are not allowed to look at anyone else's baby. This is to give the families some degree of privacy.

At Benjamin's crib, we are allowed to sit on two stools that have been placed next to his bed. Benjamin is the last baby on the left on the critical care side, farthest from the window. The nurse explained to us what was going on and answered our questions.

Benjamin is doing exceptionally well. He is still under a little oxygen hood, but every thing else is perfect. The medicine that he is getting for his heart is working great. We aren't allowed to hold him because he is hooked up to several machines. Nicki and I make up for it by holding each other.

He is so little. He weighed 5 pounds, 4 ounces at birth, but some of that was fluid. The nurse told us that his actual weight was closer to 3.5 pounds. Compared to the other babies in the critical care unit Benjamin is huge, but to me he seems as tiny as a puppy.

He didn't open his eyes during our visit, but we were allowed to touch him. The nurses told us not to overstimulate him by patting him or rubbing him because it could cause him to go into shock.

When *I* recovered from the shock of hearing that important bit of information, the nurse showed me how to place my hand on his chest. This was my first act as a father.

There is so much to learn. It is uncomfortable sitting in this large, open room trying to visit Benjamin. The room is extremely bright and unbelievably loud. Each monitor makes a distinctive sound. The noise is very distracting.

There is also a lot of traffic around the workstations. In addition to a steady stream of visitors, the doctors, nurses, and therapists are in constant motion. It is overwhelming.

Nicki and I visited Benjamin for over an hour. She is still recovering from the delivery and stress of the past several days and is tiring. She doesn't want to leave Benjamin, but Dr. Roussis told me to make sure she takes it easy. I have convinced

EARLY ARRIVAL

her to leave by telling her that the grandmothers are anxious to start spoiling the newest member of our family.

The fear we have experienced during this past week has been erased. Seeing Benjamin in his crib rather than his image on an ultrasound screen makes everything seem OK.

I have no idea how long Benjamin will need to be here. I don't think the doctors will let us take him home until they are sure his heart is OK. That might take as much as a couple of weeks.

I still don't know the name of Benjamin's doctor. One came by and introduced himself to us, but it was like meeting someone at a party. I forgot his name as soon as he said it because I was so focused on Benjamin.

We told the grandparents that they were in charge as we got on the elevator to go back to Fort Sanders Hospital. The orderly and I lugged Nicki back up through the tunnel. A friend of ours was waiting in Nicki's room when we got back. He brought news that everybody at home was praying for us. He also brought Benjamin's first present — a little outfit and a stuffed toy.

I'm starting to feel that a lot of firsts are in store for us. That's OK because beginnings are a lot better than endings.

FEBRUARY 27

DR. ROUSSIS TOLD NICKI that she could go home. That means we will have to drive back and forth to the hospital to see Benjamin. I have decided to take a couple of weeks off from work. By that time, Benjamin should be home.

I took everything home that had been at the hospital while Nicki stayed with Benjamin. I hung an "It's a Boy" sign over the door to the nursery so that Nicki will see it tonight when she comes home.

On the way back to the hospital, I realized that I am really excited. I want to see Benjamin. It doesn't even bother me that he is still at the hospital because it will let me ease into parenthood.

When I got to the nursery, Nicki and her mother were sitting by Benjamin's crib. I can see them from the observation window. I caught Judy's eye and she left so that I could go into the nursery. As we pass in the scrub-in room, she filled me in about the day's events. A doctor has been by to tell Nicki that it looks like Benjamin's heart is going to be fine — the SVTs have stopped. Benjamin's weight is going down, but this is of no concern because it was to be expected. He had retained a lot of fluid before his heart rhythm converted. We still can't hold him, but that will come soon — maybe as early as tomorrow. The doctor thinks all is well.

As we sat beside Benjamin's crib in the nursery, I noticed how open everything is. Everyone seems so exposed. Some of the babies aren't doing well. You can see it in the faces and demeanor of their parents. Since the room is so open, there is no place to go for privacy.

I am just happy that Benjamin is doing all right. I don't care if it will be a week before I get to hold him. I can wait.

F E B R U A R Y 2 8

AT 8:35 P.M., NICKI AND I HELD BENJAMIN for the first time. He is doing so well that the doctors have removed the oxygen hood. The nurse placed our son into Nicki's arms. Nicki cried, of course, but I couldn't do anything but grin. I had worn my Scrooge McDuck sweatshirt tonight to celebrate the occasion.

Benjamin is still listed in serious condition, but that appears to just be a precaution. There is a cuff taped around his foot to measure his heart rate and the oxygen saturation in his blood. He also has a feeding tube attached. Everything else has been removed.

During the scrub-in, I met the father of a little baby girl named Emily. Her bed is directly across the aisle from Benjamin. Emily was born at only twenty-four week's gestation and she could have fit in the palm of my hand. Emily's dad is about ten years younger than I am. While Nicki was holding Benjamin, I couldn't help but watch him look at Emily.

Emily is his first child, and because of complications with her pregnancy, his wife has not yet been able to come for a visit. Emily barely weighed one pound. The doctors have wrapped her bed with cellophane because her skin has not yet developed. Just the rush of air caused by someone passing in front of her bed could be too much stimulation for her.

Emily is the only girl in Stage I. Because girls develop faster, they are less likely than boys to have severe respiratory problems. Emily looks bad. A machine is breathing for her. Although I'm sure he didn't realize it, her dad began timing his breaths with those of the machine.

Emily's nurse is named Nancy. Since Emily seemed to be the sickest baby in the nursery, I assume that Nancy must be one of the best nurses. Dr. Howick came by and talked to Emily's dad. Although I tried not to listen, I heard what he said.

Their conversation made watching Emily's father so much harder. He was looking for something to hold onto, but there was nothing for him to grab. He just sat there and looked at his daughter.

It would have been so easy for the doctor or the nurse to give him hope, but they didn't. They were preparing him for something he knew, but could not yet believe. His daughter is going to die — maybe not tonight or tomorrow, but she would never go home. All of the talks that he and his wife had about how to raise her, who she would take after, what she would become, are bitter epitaphs for a child who to everybody but her parents will be just a name.

As I watched this man, I knew that he did not know how to say goodbye to a baby he would never hold. I wondered if they had finished her nursery. I thought about how hard it would be to go home after everything was over and have to see that nursery.

I wish I could to go over to his house and put everything away — paint the walls white — erase every reminder of this little girl Emily — but how do you forget her name?

I will forget what Emily looks like, and there won't be many other memories of her, but her name will always be there.

After Emily's dad went outside, I started reading a story to Benjamin from a book about Winnie the Pooh. I tried to read quietly, but Nicki asked me speak up so that Emily could hear, too. As I finished the story, I looked over and saw Nancy, Emily's nurse, smiling at me. I hope Emily heard that story. Tonight I'm going to pray that when Emily gets to heaven she will meet my Mamaw. Mamaw would have loved to see me with my own child. Until Mamaw meets Benjamin, maybe Emily will tell her about the story I read to him, just like she used to read to me.

Emily did not make it through the night.

MARCH 1

BENJAMIN WAS FED for the first time today. This involved putting a teaspoon full of formula in a syringe and holding it up so it would flow into his stomach. Nicki was so excited she almost exploded!

The doctors told us that if Benjamin keeps improving, he might come home as soon as three to four weeks from now — a little longer than I would like, but workable. I learned that babies do not develop any faster outside of the womb than they do inside. Benjamin was two months early when he was born and would not start behaving like a newborn baby until his due date — or until the later part of April.

The nurses tucked him into an oval cushion to simulate the womb. He doesn't do much more than lie there curled up in a fetal position while we watch him.

As I became more comfortable with Benjamin's condition, I began to notice the eleven other babies in our section. Coulter is the star of the nursery. His bed is directly in front of the visitor's window. He is the first baby you notice when you enter the nursery.

The only African-American baby in the NICU is Brandon and he is not doing well. He has already had several surgeries. His stomach is distended.

Each one of these babies and their parents has a different story. Most of these people I would never have met. But at this time in our lives, we are together — sharing this moment.

M A R C H   2

NICKI HAD A WONDERFUL VISIT with her father and Benjamin today. Benjamin has been moved to Stage II — a major step toward going home. One of the neat things about being in Stage II is that a nurse does not constantly supervise us. We can pick up Benjamin any time. I have become somewhat overwhelmed now that I realize how much there is to do to prepare for Benjamin's arrival at our home.

MARCH 3

I HELD BENJAMIN FOR THE SECOND TIME today for over an hour. When I came into the nursery, I noticed that there was a Beanie Baby® named Butch™ that had found its way into his crib. My mother is a Beanie Baby® addict and had picked this one out in a tribute to our other son, J.R., a Jack Russell Terrier.

It did not surprise me to see a Beanie Baby® in Benjamin's crib. What got me was that Butch was spread out across Benjamin's head. I thought someone was playing a joke, so I moved it. But when I looked around the nursery, I saw that just about every crib had a Beanie Baby® lying across the babies' heads. I asked our nurse why the Beanie Baby® was on Benjamin's head. Her reply made perfect sense. Beanie Babies® are soft. They don't put too much weight on his head. Their gentle pressure makes a baby think that he or she is still inside of mom. I wonder if the people at ©Ty know that Children's Hospital is putting their Beanie Babies® to such good use.

― EARLY ARRIVAL ―

MARCH 4

WE HAD A LONG VISIT with Benjamin tonight, but he seems a little grumpy. I don't think he looks very well. He is sort of a khaki, grayish color.

I didn't hold Benjamin today because I didn't want to interrupt Nicki's time with him. She told me she thinks his stomach is tender.

We decided it was best to cut our visit short so that both he and we could get some much-needed rest. Today is Mom's birthday, but it went uncelebrated.

TERROR IN THE NIGHT

MARCH 5

I HAVE ONE OF THOSE DIGITAL CLOCKS with great big numbers — the kind that was popular in the 1980s — no radio, no alarm, just a clock. I paid a dollar for it when I worked at the Radio Shack during college. I've kept it because it was cheap and I like it. I sleep so lightly that I don't need an alarm. The telephone rang at 5:50 in the morning.

When I wake up in the middle of the night, the first thing I do is look at the clock. Since Benjamin has been in the hospital I have gotten into the habit of leaving a cordless telephone on the nightstand beside our bed. Things have been going so well that when the telephone rang, it both startled and terrified me at the same time.

It rang only once before I hit the button. I knew it was someone from the hospital even before I heard the doctor's voice. I also knew it was bad. I wanted it to be a crank call — a wrong number — anyone but someone from the hospital.

Our house was completely dark except for the red illumination of the clock and the light from the handset that came on when I pressed the talk button. I got that feeling you get when you are driving and you barely avoid an accident — that tingly feeling that starts just below your neck when you realize what just happened. Terror hit me hard. Please don't let it be a call from the hospital.

I answered before the second ring stopped. I could hear the panic in my own voice. As soon as Dr. Howick spoke, I felt my stomach being ripped out. Doctors can deliver bad news, at inopportune times, in deliberate fashion. Although he and I had never met, he assumed, correctly, that I would know who he was. He did not waste any time on identification or an apology for calling at that hour, but simply said his name and that Benjamin had gotten sick during the night and had been intubated. I didn't realize that this meant a breathing tube had been inserted down his throat.

Although I make my living asking questions, and feel no intimidation around doctors, my mind was a total blank. I did not think to ask what had caused Benjamin to be sick or even what type of sickness he had. All I could think of was "please don't die."

Dr. Howick never said that Benjamin could die, but that's what I heard. Over the last two weeks I had conditioned myself for Benjamin's death. This call was just confirmation of my

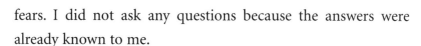

fears. I did not ask any questions because the answers were already known to me.

After I hung up, I immediately regretted that the telephone was on my side of the bed because Nicki did not suffer from the same affliction that had rendered me incapable of talking. Within the time that it took for me to hang up and roll toward her, she fired off at least ten questions, all of which were appropriate and none of which I could answer. *So I lied.*

I suppose it is bad to admit that you would lie to your wife at such a critical time. But I was rattled by the call and embarrassed by my inability to handle the conversation with the doctor. I tried to do what I felt was best, so I told Nicki that Benjamin was sick and that we needed to go to the hospital later that morning. I embellished the conversation by adding that there was no need to come immediately, omitting the reason — which was that visitors were not allowed into the NICU until 8:30 a.m.

We lay in bed, but there was absolutely no way to sleep. I couldn't even shut my eyes. I stayed completely still. I didn't even disturb the sheets. Maybe if I didn't move, it would be OK. I tried to hide in the morning darkness — to escape what was happening.

We got up around 7:30 a.m. As we showered and prepared to leave, we called our respective parents. The trip to the hospital was made in silence. Nicki and I didn't say a word to each other during the drive or on the way up to the Fifth Floor because neither one of us wanted to confront the fact that something terrible was happening. We were still getting used to the idea that we had a son. If being in shock means not having the ability to speak, feeling totally withdrawn, and having the full-body tingles, then I was in shock.

As we stepped off of the elevator at the NICU, the blinds to the unit had not yet been opened. We were the only people in the hallway. We walked in through the door that leads to the intercom and hit the button. After we identified ourselves, we were buzzed back. We scrubbed quickly and walked toward where Benjamin had been the night before.

As we turned the corner, the first thing I saw was Nicki's mother sitting by the last of the twelve critical care cribs with her head in her hands — crying. I did not see the doctor or the nurses. All I could see was Judy and that Benjamin was now in the crib where Emily had been when she died.

It was only about twenty feet from where we were to the crib, but it might as well have been a mile. As we walked, a gentleman in a suit and tie met us halfway there. He identified himself as being a chaplain. He told me that Benjamin was not doing well and he asked to say a prayer.

I am a Christian and my faith is important. I look to God and the Church for guidance concerning even minor problems, let alone a major crisis. Nicki and I knew nothing about Benjamin's condition, except that his grandmother was crying her eyes out at his bedside. My immediate reaction was to say, "Back away, Bible Man — let's give the doctors a chance to work!" Before we resorted to praying, I wanted to give medicine a chance. But for the fact that he was shielding himself with the Inspired Word of our God, I probably would have hit him —

hard. Instead, I stopped and prayed with him while Nicki went on to Benjamin's bedside.

The chaplain did not even know my son's name. He offered a fairly generic prayer for Benjamin's life — the whole time I kept thinking, "Why am I standing here with this man who has just turned my panic meter past ten to the mythical eleven?"

Nicki does not suffer from the guilt that comes from a Southern Baptist upbringing, so she totally disregarded Bible Man and sought out the doctor. By the time I arrived, she was well into a discussion with Dr. Buchheit, the neonatologist responsible for the critical care babies.

During the night Benjamin had been stricken by some sort of an infection and they were struggling to keep him alive. Benjamin's eyes were closed and he had a tube down his throat to help him breathe. His body was a tangle of wires and monitors.

Sometime during the next half hour, a nurse explained to us what all of the i.v.'s and tubes were for and that the important thing now was to determine the cause of the infection. Nicki and I sat with Benjamin and we both began to cry. We didn't talk — she just placed her hand against his chest while it rose and fell with the rhythm of the machines. I put a hand over my face to cover the tears.

I am not a crier. I can count on one hand the number of times that I have cried in my life —I especially don't cry in public. I don't believe there is such a thing as a "good" cry. But here I was sitting in a room beside my son and my wife — with everyone looking at me — crying. Dr. Prinz, the senior partner of the group that oversees the NICU, came over behind Nicki and me and hugged us both. He offered no encouragement, just a hug. As soon as I felt his embrace, I started to shake. Tears flooded from my eyes. I felt such pain, but I couldn't let it out fast enough. I lost my breath.

About 9:00 that morning the blinds to the big observation window were opened. Several members of our family had assembled outside. I couldn't look at them. I didn't want them to see me crying. I didn't want them to see me at all. If they asked me questions, I would have to tell them what was happening. I didn't know if I could say the words. So I looked down — not at Benjamin or at Nicki — just down. I covered my eyes with my hands and tried to block everything out — tried to hide.

Nicki wanted me to come with her to tell the family what was happening, but I wouldn't go. I pulled away when she took my hand. All I could say was "you go." I couldn't even watch her as she walked away.

While she was gone, I sat by Benjamin's crib. Until then, Nicki and I had always visited Benjamin together. This was the first time that he and I had ever been alone. I did not know what to do so I told him about his name and why we had chosen to call him Benjamin. I collect comic books. Mom got me started when I was little. When I was a child, she and Pop would take my sister Ann and me to the store. We each got a quarter. Ann bought candy and I bought comic books. I still buy them — by the hundreds.

TERROR IN THE NIGHT

By the time I was six years old, I was hooked. I would read them carefully and then stack them neatly in rows by titles — *Spider-Man*, *Daredevil*, and *The Avengers*. I saved my money and bought as many as I could. I took my clothes out of the chest in my bedroom so I would have a place to store them. My favorite comic book was the *Fantastic Four* and my favorite character was Benjamin Grimm, the Thing.

The Fantastic Four were Marvel Comics' first superheroes. Benjamin Grimm had super-human strength, but he was also turned into an orange, rock-skinned monster. I loved him! People were afraid of him because he was so ugly, but he had a big heart. He also had an indomitable spirit and a curmudgeon's sense of humor. He was the bravest and most loyal of all of the heroes — always the first to sacrifice himself for the good of the group — and he never gave up.

We spent months trying to come up with a name. I wanted Robert, my grandfather's name, but Nicki refused to have a child named Bob. My second choice was Atticus — after my literary idol Atticus Finch from *To Kill a Mocking Bird*. Sebastian, Samuel, and Samson were all shot down. Nicki liked yuppie names like Carter, Aaron, or Brett. We couldn't agree on anything. Finally, after five months, I told her that I had been holding back a name I loved — Benjamin. She said Benjamin was perfect.

So that is what I told Benjamin — his name is the same as my favorite comic book character. I paid a lot of money for a copy of *Fantastic Four 1* so that Benjamin could have it as a keepsake from me to him.

I also told him about myself and about Nicki. I told Benjamin about our love of movies and *Star Trek*. I talked about sports and how he had to get better so that he and I could go over to my Pop's house and watch baseball games and Tennessee football. I told him that I would teach him how to play basketball and how to fish. I told him about our dog — his dog now —J.R., our Jack Russell Terrier.

After I told Benjamin everything I could think to tell him, everything I wanted to tell him in case he died, I didn't want it to be quiet. I wanted to give him something to hold onto, a reason to live. For some reason, I decided to sing.

I am not a singer. Most of my friends and family will tell you that not only can I not carry a tune, I cannot even pick one up. I don't even sound good to myself when I sing. Someone has even given me a poster that reads "*Make a joyful noise unto the Lord, even if you're a little off key.*" But as bad as I am, I know a lot of songs. On this morning, at this time, the song I chose to sing was *He Stopped Loving Her Today* by George Jones. It's my favorite song. I sang it through ten straight times.

I would have kept on singing except that Dr. Buchheit came over to me and asked me if I had any questions. Feeling the need to be strong, I told him that I could handle bad news and that I wanted him to give it to me straight. My exact words were that I did not want him to sugarcoat it, but to tell me exactly how bad it was. Without blinking an eye, he said that I should start preparing myself because Benjamin could die.

I quickly realized that I needed this information sugarcoated and that I could not handle it. I also realized that I did not like Dr. Buchheit. He asked if I had any other questions. I did not.

From the other side of the window, Nicki saw Dr. Buchheit come up to me so she raced back in, as soon as she could scrub-in, to find out what he had said. For the second time within a three-hour span, *I lied to my wife*. I told her that Dr. Buchheit had just repeated what he told her earlier that morning.

Part of me died during the next two hours. It began when my friend Ashley came back to Benjamin's crib. The NICU is parent friendly, with two exceptions. Only parents and grandparents are allowed to come in to visit and under no circumstances are more than two people allowed at one time. Ashley was neither a parent nor a grandparent, and even though I was in a semi-catatonic state, I was able to figure out that he, Nicki, and I totaled three, not two.

I automatically assumed that this meant that Benjamin was as good as dead and that they were relaxing the rules so that Ashley could see Benjamin while he was still alive. As soon as Ashley came, I started crying again. To make matters worse, Ashley was followed by a steady procession of visitors, including my sister, another friend, Matt, and Chris, our pastor. Leigh Ann was our nurse. She never left Benjamin's side. As the day progressed, his condition deteriorated. At shift change, Andrea replaced her. By this time, Nicki and I had been at the hospital for almost sixteen hours. I felt that the best thing for her to do was to go home. She was still recovering from the trauma of Benjamin's delivery. The only way Nicki would agree to leave was if I promised to spend the night at Benjamin's bedside. In an attempt to make up for what had been a horrible husband day, I agreed. That was a mistake.

Nicki left the hospital at about 11:30. She called me when she got home and I promised again that I would call her if anything happened. *This was my third lie of the day.*

At 2:00 in the morning, Benjamin crashed.

Although parents are allowed to stay all night, no one else but me had stayed past midnight. By 12:30 a.m., even the doctor who is on call had gone to bed. Except for the nurses, I was the only other person in the room. The room still seemed brightly lit because the lights in the nursery are never turned completely off — they are only dimmed.

My medical experience is limited to what I have learned from *ER*. When Benjamin crashed, it was just like it is on television. All of the bells and the monitors went off and within seconds four nurses and a doctor were working on him. I was standing off to the side, watching everything happen. When one of the nurses saw me, she politely, but firmly, kicked me out of the NICU. For the next hour I waited in the hallway not knowing if Benjamin was alive or dead. Finally, Andrea came to get me. *Benjamin was on full life support.*

TERROR IN THE NIGHT

MARCH 6

WHEN BENJAMIN CRASHED, I was forced to leave the NICU. I tried to find a place to be by myself. The waiting room was packed, and everyone was asleep, so I lay down on the floor in the hallway outside of a doctor's office.

I couldn't get warm. I didn't have any blankets or even a pillow. The floor was cold and sleep was impossible, so I killed time by walking the hallways of the hospital, alone with my thoughts — fears actually — that when I returned to the nursery, Benjamin would be dead.

I had promised Nicki that I would call her if anything happened. Something had happened — something bad — and I didn't do anything. I balanced Nicki's need for rest with my need to not be alone. So I chose to let her sleep while I tried to get through the night by myself.

In the quiet of that early morning, I began watching a clock that hangs in the hall between the nursery and the waiting room. I leaned against the window in the corner of the hall, looking out. It was raining.

There wasn't any traffic — it was a Saturday — and I was scared. The clock hands moved so slowly that I began to wonder if the clock worked. Each minute, the big hand would suddenly jerk forward — I was that much closer to having my wife with me.

I couldn't cry. There was no one to talk to, no one to comfort me, so I waited. What was I going to tell Nicki? She had been through so much and I was going to knock her legs right out from under her. I am not strong enough to do this. Why can't it just stop?

Do prayers count when there is no hope? Can God help me? Can He save Benjamin — even when the doctors say there's nothing left to do?

I pressed my face against the glass and watched the wind whip the flag back and forth against the pole. My prayer was that God would take me and spare my child. Do I have the faith of Abraham?

The clock hand jumped again. I am one minute farther along — or closer — depending on how I chose to look at it. The quiet consumed me. No one uses the elevator, no one walks by, and nothing makes a sound, not even the clock.

I started to watch the clock even closer, trying to hear its motor, but I hear nothing. When the minute hand jumped forward, I began to wonder how accurate it was, so I started counting to myself, one-one thousand, two-one thousand, …

TERROR IN THE NIGHT

But I count too slowly. Before I got to sixty, the hand moved again. I have forgotten the moment that I started to watch that clock. Now I quit trying to anticipate its movement. I just stood there by myself — early on a Saturday morning — watching the clock.

Nicki and Judy got to the hospital early that morning, arriving just as visiting hours were ready to begin. I had to tell Nicki that Benjamin has gotten worse. She didn't have time to react because we saw Dr. Buchheit almost immediately. When we walked into the nursery, he was at Benjamin's bedside. He told us to begin preparing ourselves for the possibility that Benjamin would die this morning.

Benjamin had developed sepsis — a deadly infection. He was on full life support. The doctors had not been able to determine the cause. It was either in his bowel, his bloodstream, or his spinal fluid.

Dr. Buchheit said that if Benjamin did not begin improving soon, he would be dead by that afternoon. He was as sick as he could possibly be and still be alive.

Nicki cried and I watched. I watched Benjamin just like I had watched the clock.

The doctors began giving Benjamin a series of antibiotics that they hoped would counteract the infection. Donna is our nurse today. She is one of the experienced nurses at the nursery and she was kindly patient with our tears. She was also preparing us for Benjamin's death.

A social worker had made arrangements for Nicki and me to check into Ronald McDonald House. It was just down the street from the hospital, within walking distance. More preparation.

I had never really thought about Ronald McDonald House before. I passed it frequently, but never really understood what it was for — or what it meant.

While Nicki and Judy stayed at the hospital, I checked into Ronald McDonald House. A volunteer met me and showed me to a room upstairs. There was food provided. The only thing they asked was that we respect the privacy of the other guests. In particular, there could be no telephone calls. There was a telephone we could use to call out to Children's Hospital, but no incoming calls would be accepted. No visitors would be allowed. Ronald McDonald House was just for the families of the sickest children.

Our particular Ronald McDonald House is one of the oldest houses in Knoxville. My cousin Carol lived there when she was a student at the University of Tennessee before the Ronald McDonald Foundation purchased the property.

After I got us checked in, I drove back to the hospital. Nicki and Judy were with Benjamin and Mom and Pop hadn't gotten there yet, so I settled into the Visitor's Lounge. That afternoon I just sat at the hospital and waited. Donna encouraged us not to stay by Benjamin's bedside for too long because they had so much to do. So we waited. I waited for Benjamin to die. We waited at the hospital all day. We didn't even leave to eat.

I am so rattled by what happened last night that I cannot even go into the nursery to sit with Benjamin. I am too scared to even look through the window. I feel like I am drowning. So instead of doing something, I do nothing.

Every so often, Nicki or Judy come out to the lounge and give me an update, but nothing has changed. I picked up a *Sports Illustrated* from the waiting area and walked down the hall to the huge room where I had spent last night. I read an article about Leonard Hamilton, the former basketball coach at the University of Miami. He quoted *James 1:4*. I was so moved after reading it that I shut my eyes and prayed. I turned everything over to God. And I wait.

The waiting continues throughout the morning and into the afternoon. Every time the door to the nursery opened, I find myself tensing up, expecting the appearance of Judy or Nicki in tears with the news that Benjamin has died. At around 2:00 p.m., both Nicki and Judy came out and we tried to eat.

At 3:00 p.m., Benjamin peed. It was a miracle! Dr. Buchheit said that it was a small, wonderful step forward. The fact that Benjamin could urinate showed that his system was responding and that he was fighting the infection. The doctor did his best to not inflate our hopes, but Nicki's spirit would not be denied. She questioned him over and over. Finally, he said that, yes, this was a positive step, but that we still needed to be prepared in case Benjamin could not fight off the infection.

In the evening many of our friends came to visit. Ashley, Claudette, Jenny, Kay, and George all stopped by. I hate telling people about Benjamin being sick. I can't understand why people don't realize that each time I tell the story it takes me back to a place where I can't bear to be. It makes me weak.

I have become angry and try to distance myself from the crowd. I am so scared about Benjamin dying — about how Nicki will handle it. But I cannot escape. So I watch everybody else.

Around midnight, fatigue finally overcame us and Nicki and I went to Ronald McDonald House to try and get some sleep. There is a volunteer that stays up all night to take calls from the hospital. We were assured that if anything happens we will be told immediately.

I have not slept in almost two days. I hate feeling weak. I am not able to talk about Benjamin's situation. I don't even want to think about it, but I can think of nothing else. I want anything to hold on to, any bit of hope, anything to take this weight off me, but there is nothing.

Nicki and I called the nursery at about 2:00 that morning and were informed that there had been no change. She turned off the light and as I lay there, I looked over at another clock. It suddenly hit me that it has now been 24 hours since Benjamin crashed. It feels much longer.

TERROR IN THE NIGHT

MARCH 7

BENJAMIN SEEMS TO BE GETTING BETTER. We have not been allowed to go into to the nursery because a new baby has been brought in, but Donna comes out every thirty minutes with an excited update. Soon her enthusiasm becomes infectious, and Nicki and the grandmothers start clapping their hands every time news is delivered.

I am still not able to go back to his crib. The last time I saw Benjamin was when I was told to leave and he was put on full life support. Nicki is patient with me and does not force anything, but I don't even have the courage to look through the blinds. Dr. Nalle is on call this afternoon. As he was making his rounds, Judy asked him whether or not Benjamin was going to die. It is the question that we all wanted to ask, but haven't. He responded by saying that if he were a betting man, he would bet that Benjamin would make it. I thought there was going to be an explosion when Judy came out of the nursery to give us the news.

That gave me enough courage to go back inside the nursery. Benjamin is so small. A tube is in his throat to help him to breathe. He is connected to a tangle of wires and tubes that are everywhere. I wonder if he's really still alive. His eyes are closed and he looks sick. I put my hand on his leg like I had seen Nicki do, hoping that he knew I was with him. The nurse told us not to talk or stimulate him — that what he needed most right now was rest.

Benjamin is literally in a fight for his life. Every system in his body has shut down and the antibiotics have not yet had time to begin fighting the infection. The doctors told us that for the next couple of days, it would be up to Benjamin as to whether he would live or die.

The doctors told us that Benjamin's best chance would be if the infection had come from his bowel. If it were in his bloodstream or in his spinal fluid, he would have no chance. We will not know for two more days what was causing the infection. It would take that long for its source to be identified, so the doctors are treating him for everything.

That afternoon I settled into the waiting room, trying to watch Duke and North Carolina in the ACC finals. Our pastor came by to check on us and when I turned my head briefly to acknowledge him, a family that had stopped by for a brief visit walked in front of me and turned the channel to a NASCAR race.

I love college basketball. In particular, I love tournament basketball. I played at a competitive level and have coached our local high school team. As much as I love basketball, I really dislike NASCAR. Not only had this family been brazen enough to come into the lounge and change the channel, but also the race was in a rain delay. But for the fact that my pastor was in the room, there would have been a fight. I am not talking about saying a couple of words. I wanted real physical violence. I was so mad that I would have even hit the women.

Around 4:00 p.m., Pratt brought me a pizza from Stefanos. It would have been perfect if I could have eaten it while watching the game, but I was forced to endure a God-forsaken rain delay for almost three hours. I wish that I had been man enough to get up and turn that television off, or change it, but I remained a coward.

That night, Joey and Leslie came by for the first time. Joey is my oldest friend. We met in the third grade at Vacation Bible School and have been friends ever since. His wife Leslie is seven months pregnant. It is hard for Nicki to see Leslie because Nicki thinks that she should still be pregnant.

Joey and Leslie are great friends because none of us have expectations of the others. If we were drinkers, we would be drinking buddies. We are Democrats — they are Republicans. We live for sports — they don't even know who plays. They are the world's most patient people, while Nicki and I have the attention spans of hamsters. We love them like family. They would do anything for us.

We all sit in a circle by the big window that looks out over the street — the same window where I had watched the rain earlier — and talked about everything except what we are thinking

— is Benjamin going to die? It is surprising how people will not talk about the obvious. I suppose it is a protection mechanism.

We left the hospital that evening in far better spirits than when we arrived. We got back to Ronald McDonald House and discovered that students from Clinton High School, where I coach the Mock Trial Team, had brought hamburgers and trimmings for all of the guests. I was so overwhelmed by their kindness that I ate a double portion in an effort to fully show my appreciation.

After a late call to the nursery, we settled in for sleep. Benjamin, Nicki, and I had all made it through the day. Now it was time to rest up for tomorrow.

MARCH 8

DR. BUCHHEIT, WHO IS THE MOST PESSIMISTIC of all the doctors, told us this morning that he thought that Benjamin was going to make it. I no longer hate him. I know that he would not tell us this if he did not believe it, and I want to believe him, but Benjamin looks so sick. He doesn't move. His eyes are closed. It's as if he is dead. Maybe Dr. Buchheit just told us this because we are suffering so much.

TERROR IN THE NIGHT

There is nothing that Nicki and I can do to ease Benjamin's suffering. We can't hold him or touch him. They don't even want us to talk to him. The doctors and nurses want him to rest.

How do people live like this? Nicki and the grandparents sit all day and wait. They take turns with Benjamin — just watching. What are we supposed to talk about? I have only known Benjamin for two weeks, but I love him so much that I can't put it into words. I've only been allowed to hold him twice.

Everyone is so positive, but all I can think about is Benjamin dying. My friends, Ashley and Claudette, treat me gently when getting information, not asking questions, just letting me tell them what I want to say. I think that this is one of the reasons I love them so much — they let me talk. When I was thinking about marrying Nicki, Claudette was the first person I told. At Christmas, she helps me pick out Nicki's presents. Before I was married, she would be my "date" when Ashley had to work on the weekends. I have known Ashley for almost twenty years. I taught him how to drive. When he was fourteen years old, I gave him the keys to my car and let him drive by himself to the store. We've been like brothers ever since! It calms me to talk to them. Their first child, Riley, was born in August. With Joey and Leslie's baby due in May, I figured that Benjamin would already have two lifetime pals. What if Benjamin's life is already over?

I need someone to just listen. Nicki and my parents would, but they are hurting along with me. I need someone just for me. Someone who hurts because I do.

What does Benjamin need? Am I helping him at all? Does the fact that we sit and watch him all day make any difference or are we just doing it because there is nothing else to do?

Are Ashley and Claudette doing the same thing by just sitting with me? Is it helping them or me?

I don't have anything else to ponder today — just questions — nothing to do but sit and wait.

Every hour seems just like the hour before. It is impossible to differentiate between morning and afternoon. The same people are sitting in the same chairs. Benjamin's condition goes unchanged. Even the television in the waiting room is on CNN's *Headline News* — it repeats itself every thirty minutes.

The only thing different today is that Dr. Buchheit thinks that Benjamin will live. We repeat his words like a mantra. Every time someone asks for an update, we begin with his words.

I went with Ashley and Claudette to the elevator when they left. When the doors closed, I stood there looking at my reflection in the polished steel. What do people see when they look at me?

I have given up. I don't care what Dr. Buchheit says. I think — no, I know — Benjamin will die. I see it in my own eyes. Everyone else sees it, too.

I turned away — to go back and wait.

MARCH 9

WHEN I WAS IN COLLEGE, I ran ten miles every day. I worked out all of the time. I wanted to be able to run a four-minute mile. During my senior year in high school I was clocked at four-nineteen. Surely I could knock off twenty seconds.

So I got up every morning and I ran, not a jog, but hard running — up hills, sprints, distance.

As hard as I worked, I ran no faster. In fact, my time decreased to the point that I had to push myself to break four-thirty. Breaking a four-minute mile was beyond my ability.

Sitting at the hospital all day creates that same feeling of helplessness. There is nothing I can do. I want so much to cry — to sleep. I want to be an adult and a father. But I feel like I am nothing.

I have accepted the fact that I am just waiting for Benjamin to die. He is making no improvement. I am trying to distance myself from him. Nicki and I leave Ronald McDonald House so that we get to the hospital just as the visiting hours start. I went into the nursery with Nicki and read Benjamin's chart. I try not to look at Benjamin. I can't help it. I don't want to talk to any of the doctors or nurses. I only want to get information from Nicki.

As soon as I can, I excuse myself and I go to sit in a hallway away from all the people. I bought a newspaper and spread it out on the floor. Nicki knows where I am if she needs to find me.

The hallway where I sit is between the nursery and the neonatologist's office. The only people that use this hallway are the doctors and their staff. Dr. Buchheit has to walk around me. When we speak, it's only to exchange a short greeting. We don't talk. Nicki receives all the information.

After a couple of hours I get up and walk over to the window that looks into the nursery. It is still early and the blinds are drawn. If I press my face up against the glass, I can see through the cracks just enough to make out Nicki sitting by Benjamin's crib.

The nurse is sitting off to the side working on her notes and Nicki is alone with Benjamin. She is the only parent in this part of the nursery. She never looks up. She gently strokes Benjamin's head with the fingers of her left hand while she keeps her right hand cupped around his chest.

I watched her through the blinds for almost an hour. People walk past me, but no one speaks. Just before 11:00, a nurse pulled open the blinds. I don't want Nicki to see me, so I stepped aside. I am afraid to look at her and Benjamin. It hurts because I know that losing him will take away part of what makes her, her.

When I peek around the corner, I see that nothing has changed. The two of them have not moved. Her hands are still occupied with giving whatever comfort she can provide.

Another day passes.

MARCH 10

NICKI AND I WENT TO THE HOSPITAL the first thing this morning. Nothing has changed — more sitting. I found my corner of the hallway and settled in to wait out the morning.

Lunch does nothing to break the routine. It only serves as an interruption. I hate leaving because when we return I have to prepare myself for the news that Benjamin has died. Every time we buzz ourselves back to the scrub-in room, I fully expect a doctor or nurse to be waiting for us with sympathy and an explanation of how he died.

These times are harder than the waiting. I have gotten so worked up preparing for the news that Benjamin has died that my chest hurts — like someone is squeezing it. Part of me wishes that he would just go ahead and die so that Nicki and I can get on with putting our life back together. The rest of me is ashamed to even think these thoughts.

I want Benjamin to live or for me to be able to trade places with him. Slow deaths are inhumane, not just to the dying, but to those who are left behind.

Does life continue when your child dies? It must. Will Nicki and I have other children? Do I want to go through this again? Can I?

All of the grandparents sit in the waiting room. Nicki is with Benjamin and the two grandmothers are talking. I notice my Pop sitting in a chair over in the corner by himself.

Pop is a quiet man — introspective. It strikes me how much he loves Benjamin. When I was in college, I read an article written by a photographer for *Life* magazine. The article was about the greatest picture that he never took.

He was a young reporter when he was sent to the scene of a tragedy in a small suburb outside of Chicago. A grandfather was backing his truck out of his daughter's driveway when he ran over and killed his two-year-old grandson.

When the reporter arrived, the police and ambulance were still on the scene. The family was gathered in the living room, trying to console the young mother. The body of the child still lay in the driveway, covered by a white sheet except for a small hand protruding to the side.

As the photographer walked around to the back of the house, he saw the grandfather sitting in the kitchen all by himself. Both of the grandfather's hands were in his lap. He was alone. There was no crying, just this proud old man sitting there slumped over in a chair.

As the photographer raised his camera, the old man must have sensed his presence because he turned to look toward him. Just as the photographer was ready to snap the picture, the sorrow in the old man's eyes hit him. There was no protest, just the bitter resignation of what he had done.

The photographer lowered his camera and walked away, not out of respect for the man, but in respect for the loss.

Seeing my father sitting there, tall and straight, made me think about what strength really is. Pop was hurting as much as any of us, perhaps even more, but he was here — uncomfortable, out of place, but he was here. That's what matters.

It is this example that I try to keep in my mind when looking for something to hold onto. I need to be here for Benjamin and for Nicki. The strength comes not from the action, but from the presence.

As long as Benjamin lives, I will be here.

MARCH 11

THE NCAA TOURNAMENT STARTED today and it saves me. I watch every minute of every game. I only go to the bathroom during commercials and I dare anyone to touch the television. The tournament gives me something to do other than to sit on the floor, read newspapers, and wait for my son to die.

I love sports — basketball and baseball in particular. I love to play, to coach, to watch. My favorite thing to do is to talk about sports.

Matt, a friend who played minor league baseball, said that when he was studying to become a doctor the thing that helped him the most was the discipline he learned from being in sports. When he and Liz drop by to visit, he quickly turns the conversation to basketball. As a doctor, he is one of the few people allowed to check on Benjamin first hand. He knows how sick Benjamin really is.

Instead of trying to talk about what is happening, or to explain what Benjamin's doctors try to explain to us, Matt just wants to talk about Iowa's chances in the tournament. He is so persistent that I gave in and we began going through the brackets, making picks. While Matt and I were slamming each other's Final Four selections, Liz was doing the same thing for Nicki by talking about house plans.

For the first time in almost a week, I am thinking about something other than Benjamin dying. I feel almost normal.

After they left, I couldn't wait for the games to start. They are my release. I recorded the scores on my bracket sheet, crossing off games I picked incorrectly and circling the ones I was right about.

When Pop got there, he joined me at the television. He slammed my Final Four selections, too.

Life is coming back — slowly.

MARCH 12

THIS EVENING WE CAME BACK to the NICU after dinner and our nurse is Nancy. She was Baby Emily's nurse the night she died. I had watched Nancy work with some of the other families of the babies in the nursery, but this is the first night that she has cared for Benjamin.

As has become my custom, I went in with Nicki at the beginning of the shift to look at the chart and see if there has been an update. As Nicki and I walked back to the crib, Nancy gave us the run down. I was only half listening when she told Nicki to sit down in a rocking chair that had been placed by the crib because she needed her to hold Benjamin while she changed his bed.

Nicki immediately began crying. I felt a confidence swell up from inside me that I thought was lost. When Nancy placed Benjamin into Nicki's arms and began to change the sheets, I was overwhelmed. He was still intubated and connected to the various monitors by a tangle of wires. But somehow, Nancy was able to place him in Nicki's arms where his head rested in the bend created by her elbow.

It was so unexpected. That's what made it perfect. We came in from dinner ready to sit by the crib and watch, just as we had done for the past week. Instead, Nicki was given the responsibility of holding Benjamin while his sheets were being changed.

Finally, briefly, everything seemed OK. Nicki was crying and Nancy had a sly glint in her eyes like she was pulling a prank. I happened to catch a glance of the grandparents who were huddled around the observation window. Their mouths were wide open and they were hopping up and down with joy.

Both of the grandmothers were crying and clapping their hands. I caught my father's eye and he gave me a pump of his fist! My sister Ann was there, too, her head thrown back, laughing with joy.

Nothing different was said at this visit, and Benjamin really hadn't improved any from the morning, but getting to hold him made all the difference. It was like a shot of adrenaline.

Nicki got to hold Benjamin for a full forty-five minutes while Nancy joked with the other nurses, giving us as much privacy as we could have in a crowded nursery. I felt like part of a family.

This nurse has given me more than anyone has ever given me. She gave me a moment of peace and confidence. I have never loved a moment as much as this one.

I couldn't sit still. I would look over Nicki's left shoulder, then her right. I would reach around her to grab Benjamin's hand, careful not to pull out any wires. I was giddy.

Nicki and I must have talked, but I can't remember what we said. One hundred percent of our attention was on Benjamin.

Everyone is smiling at us. Maybe it is because we are smiling. It is the happiest I have ever been. It feels like a surprise party and I am the guest of honor!

Dr. Prinz came by and patted me on the back. He said Benjamin looked like he was doing better. I believed him.

Several of the nurses dropped by for a quick peek. All of the comments were positive. If pure unadulterated joy can cause a person to explode, then I was in serious danger.

Through all of this, Nancy just sat on her stool, keeping up a running commentary with half of the nursing staff. Every time I looked up at her, she was focused on someone else. She wasn't worried about the monitors or how Nicki was holding

Benjamin. She just went about her business like everything was fine.

When I left the NICU to let the grandmothers take a turn and started trying to answer all of the questions that were being thrown at me, I realized that there was nothing new to say because Nancy had not really told us anything. I did not know if his medicine had been changed or if they had determined the cause of the infection. I didn't really know anything except that all of a sudden it was OK for Nicki to hold Benjamin. And that was enough.

Moms are supposed to hold their babies. If Benjamin were going to die, then surely the doctors and the nurses wouldn't be this happy. Suddenly I was ashamed. I remembered the prayer I had offered after I read the Bible verse that I had found in *Sports Illustrated* — when I thought I had turned everything over to God:

> *Let patience have her perfect work so that you may be perfect and complete and wanting nothing.*
> **James 1:4**

I hadn't turned anything over to God. I had tried to keep it all inside. I had grown impatient with the waiting.

At this moment I "wanted nothing." Nancy had given me everything. I was "complete." I was going to be all right.

As I settled into my customary seat in the lounge to watch the basketball tournament, I received another positive sign. The University of Tennessee won its first NCAA tournament game in more than a decade. Today has been a good day.

TERROR IN THE NIGHT

MARCH 13

NURSE NANCY IS MY ALL-TIME FAVORITE person. She knew what Nicki and I needed most and yesterday she delivered. We never asked, and would not have even thought to ask, to hold Benjamin, although that was what we wanted more than anything. Now we can't wait for visiting hours so that we can get back to see him. I suppose that before all of this happened I thought the only thing nurses did was give shots and take your temperature. This nurse gave me back my life. It is like getting the perfect present.

My favorite Christmas growing up was the year I got an *Atari* video game. I had not dared to ask for one so it was not on my Christmas list. When I woke up that morning to see what Santa had brought, there it sat, right in front of all the presents. I played with it for hours — for years.

What made the *Atari* so perfect was that it was the thing that I wanted most. I wanted it so much that I was afraid to ask for it because of the disappointment that would come if I didn't get it.

That was the kind of feeling that Nicki and I experienced when we were allowed to hold Benjamin. We were afraid to even consider asking because we knew in our hearts that the doctors and nurses would have said no. He was attached to too many wires — he was still too sick — one of any number of excuses.

But when Nancy placed him in my arms I could feel him breathe. He was alive. I was alive.

I am holding my son. I am sitting in the same rocking chair that I sat in one week ago — on the night that they told me that Benjamin could die before morning — and now I am holding him. I love him.

He is my child — a part of me. I hate myself for giving up. I doubted my faith when my strength started to fail. When I faltered, I was carried by my wife, my family, and my friends — by God. I was carried and I didn't even know it.

TERROR IN THE NIGHT

MARCH 14

TODAY IS POP'S BIRTHDAY. I have watched every NCAA game that has been televised during the past four days including Southwest Missouri State's thumping of my beloved Vols.

Holding Benjamin has lifted our spirits so much that we decided to check out of Ronald McDonald house and spend our first night at home. Benjamin has begun to make some steady improvement. The doctors think he is moving out of danger. He is still sick, but even I can tell that he is getting better.

He is starting to move — not a lot, but enough. His eyes still haven't opened, but I think this is for the best. Maybe he won't know there is a tube in his throat.

The house seems so empty. It's quiet compared to the nursery. Nicki and I feel lost. When we are at home, we call the hospital several times during the night to check on Benjamin. Everything is fine.

When I lie down and try and to sleep, the feeling is the same as when I am at the hospital or was at Ronald McDonald

House. I don't think about anything. I just empty my mind and try to let sleep come — no memories or expectations. I just shut my eyes and lie completely still in the darkness — praying that the telephone doesn't ring — waiting for tomorrow.

MARCH 15

BENJAMIN HAD HIS FIRST HAIRCUT TODAY. There was none of the normal pomp and circumstance that usually comes with the event. The reason for the trim was that the nurses had to shave a space to put in an i.v. They kept the hair in a little plastic bag as a memento of the occasion.

One of the problems that the nurses are having is finding i.v. sites. Benjamin has been stuck so many times, and has so many tubes in him, that they are having difficulty keeping an i.v. open.

I decided to wear one of the yellow surgical masks that they provide at the scrub-in station just in case I am carrying a germ. I have never seen anyone else wear a mask, but I figured that it's better to be safe then sorry. My favorite television show while I was in law school was *Alf*. One of the characters had a saying, "Let caution be our credo." I have adopted it for when I spend time with Benjamin. No risks. The last thing he needs is a cold!

Today we got the results of Benjamin's first ultrasound of his head. The doctor used the term PVL, but I did not think to ask what that meant. Premature babies are susceptible to intraventricular hemorrhages. These are bleeds in the brain. They can be a mild Grade I up to a severe Grade IV bleed. A Grade IV can be life-threatening.

Benjamin had a Grade I bleed on the left side and a Grade II bleed on the right. The doctors said that this was not serious enough to be concerned about, but that they wanted to run another ultrasound in a week to make sure that there had been no damage.

Benjamin looks rough. My mother would say that he looks like he had been "rode hard and put up wet." He has started opening his eyes for brief periods of time. But for the most part he sleeps. He is still fully intubated. A machine is helping him breathe, but it has been cut down significantly. Even more important is that the nurses are upbeat.

Watching people's reactions is the best way to tell how things are really going. When Benjamin was at his worst, I could sense it by looking at their faces and listening to the tone of voice used by the doctors and the nurses. When things are going well, they are upbeat. The exception is Dr. Buchheit. He is difficult for me to read.

Dr. Buchheit has been assigned to Benjamin for the entire month of March so we meet with him on a daily basis. I try to watch his eyes as he gives us information, but it is difficult for me to get a feel for what he is saying. He would be a good poker player.

The night I stayed in the nursery with Benjamin when he became so sick, Dr. Buchheit was on call. Some time after midnight, the nurses were having trouble with the ventilator for the baby in the isolette nearest Benjamin.

A respiratory therapist was called in to adjust the machine. When he couldn't get it fixed, the decision was made to wake up Dr. Buchheit and call him in to check the machine. When Dr. Buchheit arrived, it was obvious that he had been asleep. As the respiratory therapist was explaining what seemed to be wrong with the machine, Dr. Buchheit didn't even acknowledge what he was saying. Instead, he pressed a button and the machine corrected itself. He turned and left — saying nothing — he just did his job.

Most people are open books to me. As a trial attorney, I make my living reading witnesses, juries, judges, and other lawyers. This man totally controls his emotions. If Dr. Buchheit is optimistic or pessimistic, I cannot tell. This has become quite frustrating for me.

Apart from that, he is an incredible physician. He is patient, especially with Nicki. She is highly intelligent and has a science background. She is not afraid to ask questions. Dr. Buchheit never makes us feel rushed and gives us detailed answers. If he does not know, he does not guess. I like him.

Nicki and I had a long discussion over dinner about what comes next. She obviously feels that the hard part is over and now it is just a matter of getting Benjamin better so that he can come home. I am not quite so optimistic. I have not been to the office in over three weeks. And I am woefully behind.

We decide that beginning tomorrow I will go to work and Nicki will go to the hospital. I will have someone take me to the hospital in the afternoon so that I can drive Nicki home at night. She will call me with updates throughout the day. That will now be our new routine.

On the drive back home, Nicki fell asleep in the car.

MARCH 16

TODAY HAS BEEN A GOOD DAY. By that I mean there were no major set-backs. I went into work early. It felt really good. I have resigned myself to the fact that Benjamin is going to be in the hospital for a long time — maybe months. As much as I hate to leave Nicki, I have to go back to work.

There is a family from Indianapolis with a baby in the nursery. They were on their way to Gatlinburg for a vacation when the mother went into labor. She was only at 29 weeks, and like Nicki, the pregnancy had been routine.

They are starting their third month in the NICU. Both parents work at hourly jobs and their family-leave time has expired. They have been forced to return to Indiana. They drive back and forth each weekend, returning for work on Monday morning. They have to drive all night just to make it on time.

I am lucky. For the most part, I can come and go as I please. The problem is that as a litigator, my calendar has been set months — sometimes years — in advance. My partners are covering for me as much as they can. Judge Scott and Chancellor Lantrip, the two judges in my district, have reworked their dockets to accommodate my absences. But still, I have to return to work.

Sal has offered to drive me to the hospital after work. He and I grew up together. We were roommates in college and now are law partners. He is a tall, handsome Italian. He can sing, dresses like a model, and drives a Viper. Where I live, he is our most eligible bachelor.

Today, however, he was my chauffeur. Before going to the hospital, he stopped at the high school so that he and I could scrimmage against the basketball team.

It felt good to run — to sweat. The coaches gave us a hard time for being so out of shape. Locker rooms are not places where you get coddled. The entire coaching staff knows how sick Benjamin is, but I get no pity on the court — that's the way it should be.

I don't want people to treat me differently. I'm still me.

My life is starting to come back, but I am still too scared to let myself believe that everything will work out. I refuse to be optimistic or to let my guard down. I am still shaken by that night Benjamin crashed.

It's hard being so cautious. It's frustrating watching the normality of everyone else's life knowing that every telephone call could be a message that Benjamin has died.

No one had ever spoken to us about possible complications with Nicki's pregnancy. And I had never known anyone who had a premature baby. All of my friends brought their babies home in just a couple of days. What happens to us next month or the month after?

My accountant, Gary, had a premature son. They were in Children's Hospital for several weeks. He tried to talk to me about what is going on, but I'm not ready yet. I have thousands of questions, but I want Benjamin to get more stable.

Without saying anything, he knows what I'm going through, so he doesn't push me.

On the way to the hospital, Sal broke the speed of sound. I found myself holding onto the dash. If he is trying to get my mind off of Benjamin, it worked.

When I arrived at the nursery, Nicki was upbeat. She filled me in on the day's events. There has been some progress, but not enough to change our course any.

During the drive home I told her about everything that I've done today. It's the most we've talked in days. We talk about our lives, not just Benjamin.

Today is a good day.

MARCH 17

HAPPY ST. PATRICK'S DAY! Benjamin came off the ventilator! Nicki called me from the hospital this morning and I rushed to see him. I actually urged Sal to drive faster. I can hardly walk because I am so stiff from playing basketball yesterday, but I don't care.

I am a full-blooded Irishman. For Benjamin to come off the ventilator on an Irishman's holiday is perfect. Nicki and I went to Tuscany's to celebrate.

Tuscany's is our favorite restaurant. Our first date was at Tuscany's — I proposed to Nicki at Tuscany's — and every major holiday is celebrated at this restaurant. We had not been there for several months. Once I got the good news about Benjamin, there was no doubt about where the evening would be celebrated.

Since Benjamin is off the ventilator, we are allowed to hold him. During the visit he opened his eyes. His skin is flaked and dry because they keep a heat lamp on him to keep him warm.

The nurses haven't been able to bathe him because of the breathing tube.

His eyes show that he has been in a battle and that he has survived. One of the nurses took a picture of him surrounded by his stuffed animal friends. His eyes are wide open, telling the story about what a rough week he has had.

When he gets older, I will show him this picture as a reminder of the week that his father and mother had. Then I will hold him tight, like I'm not going to let go. I love my son and I will tell him that every day.

MARCH 18

I HAD A LONG VISIT AT THE HOSPITAL. Everything is looking great. My muscles still hurt from playing basketball yesterday, but everything is so positive that I can't help but feel good. Benjamin is like a different baby. He acts like he feels better.

He wakes up when Nicki and I visit. He looks around. I'm sure he recognizes Nicki's voice. He even stretches his arms and legs.

Since he is no longer intubated, the nurses are a lot more lenient in letting us hold him. We can count on at least one extended cuddle session per visit.

The doctors told us Benjamin's eyes haven't started to focus yet — that he can only see about a foot in front of his face. I get as close as I can so that he can see me. I'm still wearing a mask. Benjamin probably thinks I'm Spiderman.

During our visit we laugh. I can't remember the last time I laughed. Suddenly everything is funny. I cracked more one-liners than Henny Youngman. What's even funnier is that Nicki and the younger nurses have no idea who Henny Youngman is. That makes me laugh again.

I look forward to going to the hospital. The helplessness I felt last week is gone. So is the desperation.

It's after 2:00 a.m. before we even think about going home. Benjamin is going to live. Nobody has to tell me that because now I believe it.

Nicki and the grandparents knew it all along. So did Benjamin. Now I believe, too. I'm going to be a dad for a long time.

TERROR IN THE NIGHT

MARCH 19

I WENT TO THE HOSPITAL WITH NICKI this morning. We had an 8:30 meeting with the doctor. The Mock Trial team left yesterday to compete for the State Championship in Nashville. I feel selfish for wanting to leave Benjamin, but I really want to go.

I have coached the Clinton High School Mock Trial team with Kay Davis and Susan Fowler for several years. We have developed one of the most successful programs in the country. Each year, over 10,000 teams compete for a National Title. Clinton has finished second and fifth in two of the last three national competitions.

We have also won two of the last three State Championships. I really want to go. But I am afraid to leave Benjamin. Nicki tried to talk me into going. It was not until Dr. Buchheit assures me that everything is looking great, and I should go, that I agreed to leave.

After we got the go-ahead from Dr. Buchheit, Nicki practically forced me to leave. She will spend the night with her mother. It was hard for me to leave them, but I made the two and a half hour drive to Nashville to meet the kids in time for the first round.

Before bed check, I led a devotional with the team. I told them about Benjamin. I showed them pictures and told them about the past month and how my faith has been tested and tried.

I find that I pray constantly — not just for Benjamin, but for everything. I pray for others. I pray for strength. I start each morning with a prayer. I try to remember to be thankful for everything. I pray for guidance and for compassion. As I was standing in line to get into the courthouse, I said a prayer of thanksgiving for no rain. I love praying.

Empathy is something that I've never had much of before. I think lack of empathy for each other's struggles is one of our greatest short-comings.

Has Benjamin taught me this?

Tonight I slept alone in a hotel bed and realized how much I needed this time away from the hospital. I watched *Sports Center*, twice. I ordered a pizza. I turned the air down as low as it would go. I took a long, hot shower and got in bed — naked. Then I ordered a movie and settled in for the night. I have a lot to pray for.

MARCH 20

WE WON OUR THIRD STATE CHAMPIONSHIP in four years! The kids were phenomenal. I left the celebration and drove back to Knoxville in a driving rain. As I came over the Cumberland Plateau, I could barely see ten feet in front of me. It rained all the way from Nashville to Knoxville.

I saw a sign at the Crossville exit for a *Krystal* restaurant. I did not want to take the time to stop and eat because I wanted to get back to the hospital so I decided I would get a bag of Krystals and eat them as I drove.

The mayor of the city of Crossville should be beaten. There is, in fact, a *Krystal* restaurant at that exit, but you have to drive over twenty minutes to get to it!

Once I got off the Interstate, I kept driving, and driving, and driving, thinking that I had to come across it sometime — that it couldn't be much farther. I had no idea that it would be over fifteen miles. That detour for a bag of hamburgers cost me almost an hour.

I didn't get to the hospital until around 10:00 that evening. I had a great visit with Nicki and Benjamin. I am literally exhausted from the stress of the drive, the competition, and being away from my family, but I love it. It's a good kind of exhaustion.

Nicki is excited to have me back and tells me about everything that has happened. We leave one of the cars in Knoxville and I rode back home with her. This time, I was the one who fell asleep in the car.

MARCH 21

WE HAD ANOTHER GOOD VISIT TODAY. Everything is still improving and there is a chance that Benjamin may get to eat tomorrow. That is the next thing we are waiting for — to see how he tolerates formula.

MARCH 22

NO FEEDING TODAY. Dr. Buchheit does not think Benjamin is ready.

Benjamin has taken a small step backward. We also have the results of the cranial ultrasound. The bleeds are no better.

Dr. Buchheit told us that we should not be upset about this backward step — that this is common. He says that for every two steps forward, premature babies take one step back. I take him at his word. He has not been wrong yet. I can wait.

MARCH 23

NICKI CALLED ME AT WORK IN TEARS. She broke down on the telephone. She could not tell me what is wrong, but I knew that it is bad. She wanted me to come to the hospital as fast as I could get there.

Pratt drove me to Knoxville. Nicki was sitting beside Benjamin's crib crying. One of the nurses was trying to comfort her. Nicki told me that an occupational therapist had come by to explain to her about PVL. It stands for periventricular leukomalacia — cerebral palsy. The therapist had given Nicki an article about the effects of cerebral palsy. It is devastating.

According to the article, kids with cerebral palsy cannot speak or move. This is more than Nicki can stand.

When Dr. Buchheit saw me, he came over and explained to me that Benjamin only has a mild form of CP. He said that the ultrasound shows that the PVL is located on the right side of his brain and that it should only affect the fine motor skills in his left arm.

TERROR IN THE NIGHT

He told me that there are several degrees of cerebral palsy. The occupational therapist had given Nicki information that dealt with a worst-case scenario. He felt that Benjamin, at the worst, had only a mild form of CP.

I am able to talk to Nicki and actually support her for once during this ordeal. Several of my clients have brain injuries and I know just enough to make me dangerous. I explained to her what this means and that this is workable. She reacts positively, but she is obviously devastated to learn that her child has cerebral palsy after everything else that he has been through.

All through the pregnancy, I worried about Benjamin's health — would he have Down syndrome, would he be retarded, would he have a birth defect? To learn that your child does, in fact, have a lifelong problem is devastating.

Putting it in perspective, it could be so much worse. Two months ago if you had told me that my child would have a mild form of cerebral palsy, it would have destroyed me. Now, it is almost as if it is no big deal. He has survived so much that I cannot believe that he will not fight through this, too. It makes me appreciate all the small gifts that I so often take for granted.

Tonight Nicki went to her first baby shower. It is in Sevierville at her mother's house. I didn't go. Instead, I had dinner with Jeff at the Pizza Hut.

Jeff and I coach the girls' volleyball team at Anderson County High School. I love to coach. It's exciting. The players are dedicated young women. Jeff and I made plans for the spring volleyball season while Nicki attended our first baby shower.

Nicki has been upset about all of the baby showers being cancelled. She felt that this was everyone's way of giving up. I have not been overly worried about the PVL or the threat of cerebral palsy. I think it hit Nicki so hard because of all that we've been through. The shower lifted her spirits a great deal.

I called the hospital to check on Benjamin. Our nurse tonight is Lisa. It's reassuring to know she is a military nurse. It has been my experience that people with a military background are extremely well prepared.

I called her about twenty-five times before going to bed. Not once does she tell me to stop acting like a baby. She answered my questions and put me at ease. I think she and I are going to be friends.

MARCH 24

NICKI GOT AN APOLOGY from the occupational therapist, who admitted she did not know much about PVL but had merely pulled an article off of the Internet — an article that presented only the worst-case scenarios.

She must have been reprimanded by one of the doctors or nurses because she apologized for panicking Nicki. This lifted our spirits tremendously. I have now made it my mission to learn as much as I can about PVL.

MARCH 25

TODAY IS MY BIRTHDAY. I got my first gift from Benjamin — a money clip. Nicki took me to see the movie *Rushmore* and then to Grady's for dinner.

For some reason, the only thing that I am able to keep in my stomach is soup. I don't eat anything for breakfast and I have only soup for lunch and dinner. When we make our restaurant selections, our choices are made by what type of soup they have.

Nicki is frustrated. Benjamin has gotten to the point where he is so close to getting better. She wants him to come home. I do not tell her, but this is the last thing I want. I am not ready. Her strength is almost gone. She gets up early every morning to go to the hospital and stays there until 1:00 or 2:00 the next morning when we drive home together. Eighteen- and twenty-hour days are hard.

There is nothing to divert her attention. She just sits by Benjamin's crib. He is still not taking any feedings yet. There is little for her to occupy herself with during the visits.

All I do is wait with her and eat soup.

MARCH 26

I TOOK THE DEPOSITION OF A NEUROSURGEON that I know today. Prior to the deposition, I cornered him in his office and he spent over half an hour educating me about PVL. The news was encouraging. He explained to me that the earlier the disease is diagnosed, the quicker they can begin treatment and the less likely it is that Benjamin will have any long-lasting effects.

He took a cup of water and poured it over his hand. He said that that is how the brain sends impulses to the body. It is like water sliding through the fingers — there are definite routes through which the information travels.

PVL causes some of those routes to be shut off which prevents some of these messages from getting to a portion of the body. He then held two of his fingers together and poured the water through. He explained that even though a route was now closed off, the water could still get through.

He said it was like a stroke victim having to relearn how to talk or walk. The ability is still there, the brain just has to be taught that it can still do it.

The reason that brain and spinal cord injuries are so devastating is that the body does not create any new neurological tissue. When we have a brain injury or a spinal injury, it is usually permanent, but babies continue to grow spinal tissue and brain matter up until they are about six months old. This meant that anything Benjamin had lost could be regained. Also, the PVL would not affect his intellectual capacity, it would just mean that we have to re-educate his muscles.

He told me of a patient that had over 60% of the gray matter of his brain removed. Today, that child was 10 years old and functioned completely normally. It took several years of physical therapy to get him to this point, but to look at him and talk to him now, you would not know that most of his brain was missing.

Nicki had a long visit with Dr. Howick. He gave her a goal sheet. When it is completed, Benjamin could come home. This was a good dose of "mama" medicine. The doctors and the nurses in the NICU are excellent about sensing our mood because whenever we get down, they give us something to perk us up.

This evening my family celebrated our "group birthday" at the Chop House. Mom, Pop, and I were all born in March. And my sister was married in March, so we usually pick one day to celebrate each event at the same time.

They accompanied us back to the hospital and Pop went back to see Benjamin for the first time since he got so sick. While Pop was back there, my mother told me that this has been very difficult for him.

Pop tears up whenever he talks about Benjamin. He loves Benjamin, but has such a hard time showing his emotion.

Mom tells me that the reason that he would not go back is that he couldn't stand to see Benjamin lying in the bed with the tubes in his throat. It makes me seem so selfish that I have been worrying about how I've been feeling, not realizing how much this has affected everyone around me.

I love my family.

MARCH 27

BENJAMIN IS NOT DOING WELL TODAY. We had a great visit, but I can see that he is beginning to get sick again. Dr. Buchheit told us that they are going to do another series of blood cultures to check the status of the infection.

Nicki and I went to see *Analyze This* as a break between visits. The 6:00 to 8:00 break is a great time to see a movie and grab a bite to eat. It gives us a diversion.

I sense that we should be getting ready to go back into battle.

MARCH 28

WE MET WITH DR. PRINZ TODAY. He told us that Benjamin is not improving to his satisfaction and he suspects that he is ultimately going to need bowel surgery for a condition called NEC. This is a disorder of sick premature infants that occurs when a section of either the small or large intestine is damaged or dies. NEC does not always kill all of the tissue in a particular area of the intestine. This makes it difficult to diagnose.

The neonatologists will proceed cautiously with the feeding strategy because the feeding may be a contributing factor to the NEC. In research that I did, I discovered that over 4000 babies a year suffer from NEC.

The primary cause of NEC is an infection. Since the entire intestine does not die, there is a small chance that the dead portion of the bowel will not have to be removed in order to become healthy again. The onset of NEC is slow.

The treatment is to stop the feedings and provide Benjamin's nutrition intravenously. The doctors began prescribing intravenous antibiotics and have been monitoring Benjamin each day with X-rays. The danger with NEC is that it has the potential to progress rapidly. Benjamin could develop a perforation of the intestine that will require surgery. The dead portion of the intestine will have to be removed.

It is Dr. Prinz's opinion that Benjamin is going to need the bowel surgery. He told us that we need to begin preparing for this. He also told us that this was not a particularly dangerous surgery and that it was rare that a child dies from NEC. This is yet another gut punch, but for some reason, we are not immediately horrified by the thought of the surgery.

It seems like these hard days are never going to end.

We went to see a terrible movie called *Forces of Nature*. The highlight of the night was when we got back. A card was waiting for us on Benjamin's crib from Coulter's mom, Coby. I think the only people who really appreciate what we are going through are other parents in the NICU. We are beginning to form relationships with the families around us.

Robert and Coby, Coulter's parents, are close to mine and Nicki's ages. Robert works for his family's insurance agency and Coby is a speech therapist. Coulter is their first child and he was born within days of Benjamin. Coulter is much smaller than Benjamin. The doctors have told them that because of an intraventricular hemorrhage that they are probably going to have to put a shunt in his brain which will be permanent and will grow with him.

It is therapeutic just having someone to share experiences with. Even though Coulter has been moved to Stage II, the feeling that I have is that Coulter has several serious health complications.

More, now than ever, I realize that everything is relative.

MARCH 29

BENJAMIN HAD A ROUGH NIGHT. We met with Dr. Buchheit early this morning. He informed us that the surgery would have to be performed on Benjamin's bowel to repair damage from the NEC sometime before the end of the week. Also, at 9:00 this evening Benjamin had to be intubated again.

It was like all of the air had been let out of our balloon. This is never going to end. I want to scream, hit, yell — anything to make all this stop. I pray. I cry. I think I die a little bit every morning.

MARCH 30

TODAY HAS BEEN THE ROUGHEST DAY in a long time. All I do is worry about Benjamin. When I saw him this afternoon he looked terrible. Nicki looks worse.

We met Dr. Wooldridge who will be taking over from Dr. Buchheit. He is older than Dr. Buchheit and does not talk to Nicki as much.

I have had two bad dreams in the past two nights about car wrecks. I am scared.

Nicki met with the surgeon this morning. He refused to do the operation. He did not feel that it was appropriate and told the neonatologist that they would have to wait. This made me furious.

Three different neonatologists have told us that we need to be preparing ourselves for surgery, but this surgeon refused to do it. He wants to observe Benjamin for a few more days.

Nicki and I want Benjamin to have the surgery just so we can make some sort of progress.

TERROR IN THE NIGHT

MARCH 31

TODAY WAS OUR LAST DAY with Dr. Buchheit. We had a great morning visit with Benjamin and Dr. Buchheit told us that Benjamin was improving and there was now a chance that he would not have to have the surgery.

It is hard to tell Dr. Buchheit goodbye. Nicki and I have grown to rely on him to give us the strength to continue on. We trust him and love him. He saved Benjamin's life.

I asked him if he remembered the talk he and I had when I asked him to "give it to me straight." He did. I asked him why he was so stern with me. He said, "While I certainly hoped and believed that Benjamin was going to improve and respond to what we were doing for him, I knew that there was a possibility that might not happen and felt you should be aware of it." Dr. Buchheit went on to tell me that this is always one of the most difficult conversations he has with parents, but that he didn't think it was fair to hide things from them. He also said that my reaction was exactly what he had expected — total shock.

Dr. Buchheit wants to send Benjamin to have a CT scan of his stomach. This means Benjamin will have to travel from the NICU to where the CT scans are done. Nicki went with him. They hooked him up to an isolette with "Roadrunner" written on the side.

While they were gone, he ran out of oxygen and they had to "bag" him with a hand-held breathing device. It has a part attached to the mask that is a lot like a bag . This horrified Nicki, but the nurses seemed to think that it was no big deal.

We did not get into see Benjamin until 10:30 tonight. The worst part about being on the critical care side is that we are not allowed to go into the nursery when a new baby arrives. When we showed up at 8:00, at normal visiting hours, we were informed that a new baby had just been brought into the nursery. This means we will have at least a two-hour wait. We did not get to see Benjamin until 10:30. And we did not get home until 3:00 the next morning.

None of that mattered though because while we were there, Benjamin had a bowel movement. A small, but wonderful, little spot of poop showed up in his diaper. This was a sign that the bowel was not completely dead. It was a huge step toward not having to have surgery. Suddenly, I did not hate that surgeon nearly so much. I began to pray for another bowel movement.

I am getting an incredible amount of ribbing from my friends and family about this new situation — hoping for a bowel movement — because of my own history. When I was in the sixth grade, my family went to Daytona Beach on vacation.

TERROR IN THE NIGHT

We went to *Morrison's Cafeteria* where I gorged myself on food. That night on the boardwalk I ate everything in sight. When we began to make the trip back to the motel, traffic was at a standstill.

I was sitting in the back seat of my parents' gray 1972 Dodge Polaris when all of a sudden I had a terrible poopie pain. I told Mom that she had to stop so I could go to the bathroom. Mom turned around, saying we would be at the motel within minutes and that I would just have to wait — not the answer I needed.

This poopie pain was so severe that I could not hold it. My meal at Morrison's made a reappearance. The immediate reaction of my mother, father, and sister was to roll down the windows. All I could do was cry. The harder I cried, the more I pooped. By the time I got to the motel, I was covered with poop. When we arrived, the parking lot looked like Mardi Gras. College students were everywhere and music was playing when here came my mother and father's huge Dodge Polaris, parking right next to a group of about ten people.

As I stepped out of the car in my matching Hawaiian outfit, two large clumps of poop that had been in the legs of my shorts fell to the parking lot. Everyone's attention was immediately focused on me. All I could think to do was run. I ran up the stairs to our room, leaving a little poopie pancake on every step.

The fable of the poopie pain has haunted me ever since. It has become a fitting tribute that Benjamin would have so much difficulty doing something that his father can do so easily.

THE LONG WAY HOME

APRIL 1

BENJAMIN WILL GET TO COME HOME *this weekend!* This is going to be my April Fool's Day joke. I am going to tell everyone who asks me how Benjamin is doing that the doctors are so impressed with his progress that they are going to release him sometime over the weekend.

Sal shuttled me to the hospital late in the afternoon. Nicki and her mom had already left for the day, so I got to spend some time alone with Benjamin before dinner. While I was there, Nicki called to check in and I pretended to be a nurse and took the call. When Nicki asked how everything was going, I attempted my best accent and said that he was doing great and that his release orders were being signed. The nurses and staff who were within earshot thought I was hilarious. Nicki was not amused.

Our nurse today is Esther. Although Esther is married to an Irishman, she was raised in Panama. Esther is one of the best-liked nurses in the NICU. She is Nicki's favorite daytime nurse. I am much closer to the nighttime nurses because I am only able to visit briefly during the late afternoon after work. My daytime visits usually consist of scrubbing in, reading the chart, and getting the quick rundown of the day's activities before visiting hours are over. Thanks to Sal, I arrived at the hospital early today and settled in for a fairly long visit.

Esther and Nicki became friends when Esther put robot sheets on Benjamin's bed. She told Nicki that since Benjamin was such a bright little boy, he needed to have robots on his sheets rather than regular hospital sheets.

Esther is responsible for all of the decorations in the nursery. For St. Patrick's Day, she put a clover at the top of each babies' crib with their name on it and hung leprechauns and green all throughout the nursery. Now that the Easter season is approaching, the clovers have been replaced with Easter eggs. Paper bunnies and chicks are everywhere.

It's hard to believe that it's already April. I would have forgotten the month change except that Jayme, who works with me, celebrates her birthday on April Fool's Day. When Benjamin was born, I thought that he would already be home by now. Instead, two times during the last six weeks I have had to prepare myself for the possibility that he would die. I cannot stand the thought of having to go through that again.

Nicki refuses to talk about Benjamin dying. Before he was born, before I held him, before I had seen anything except his outline on an ultrasound, Nicki would not allow us to even consider the possibility that Benjamin could die. Her mother and I spoke briefly about how Nicki would handle losing a child, but neither one of us dared bring up the subject with Nicki because those thoughts, or words, were not allowed. Nicki's child would not die.

Sitting at his bedside, watching him sleep, I think about his mother and how she, as much as the doctors or the nurses, is responsible for Benjamin's survival. What we are going through is hard, but it would be much harder to lose him.

Benjamin's head is turned slightly toward me. He has to lie on his back because of the tubes and wires. The nurses turn his head to the right and left periodically trying to make him more comfortable.

Benjamin looks so much like Nicki. Watching him makes me think about all the times, early in the morning, when I have watched her as she slept — before she wakes. Benjamin has that same look. His eyes push out against his eyelids and his lashes are long and curved. His upper lip is full with a pronounced cleft just under the nose. Just like Nicki, his cheekbones are high. I think that he is going to have my mouth, but he definitely has Nicki's eyes. I can't tell yet about his ears.

A truly beautiful person has perfect ears, and if they don't, then they're not beautiful. You can't hide ugly ears. Big ears, or ears that stick out perpendicular to a person's head, immediately draw your attention. Even worse are long ears, or ears that are scaly, or ears with a lot of hair growing out of them. Whenever I talk to someone, my eyes are drawn to their ears. Most of the time, hair or a hat cannot hide ugly ears and there is no makeup that will cover them. Beautiful ears go unnoticed. They blend in with the profile so perfectly that they become invisible, just like a great referee disappears within a game.

Benjamin's ears must be perfect because no one ever mentions them. Today is the first time that I have ever allowed myself to study them. I know that there is a certain amount of prejudice that goes with being a father, but I feel that he is truly a beautiful child. Angelic. Just like his mother.

Halfway through my visit, my parents stopped by. Mom came in to see Benjamin while Pop waited in the lounge. Benjamin is their second grandchild. My sister's son Adam is their first.

I have not been doing a good job of keeping them informed about Benjamin's progress. While we were sitting by his crib, Mom placed her hand on Benjamin's chest like she had seen Nicki do. Benjamin reached up with his right hand and grasped her finger. Mom tested his grip by gently raising her finger up and down while Benjamin held on. As I grew to adulthood, I lost count of the times that I have held onto my mother for strength.

Mom was diagnosed with cancer when I was in the seventh grade. The prognosis was not good. Ann and I were not allowed to go to the hospital to visit her because we were too young. Before her surgery, Mom sat Ann and me down on the couch. She told us that she had cancer and that she was going to need surgery. I did not know anything about cancer except that John Wayne died when he got it.

THE LONG WAY HOME

On the day of the surgery, my aunts came and stayed with Ann and me while Pop was at the hospital. I remember my Aunt Margie answering the telephone when Pop called to give her the results of the surgery — and to tell her that the tumor was malignant. Aunt Margie started crying while she was still talking on the telephone.

I got up and ran to my room, not wanting to listen as my aunts discussed the information between each other like Ann and I weren't supposed to know what was happening. But she was our mother! So I ran from the room because it terrified me to see them cry. Adults only cry about death. They can take pain or not getting their way, but death always brings tears — even when it is expected.

I locked the door and started to clean my room. I made my bed and straightened my closet until everything was arranged — perfectly — totally symmetrical. I even picked up the small white specks that the vacuum cleaner doesn't pick up. Then I turned off the lights and sat between the wall and my bed.

I could not imagine living without my mother. She was my best friend. She taught me how to read and she shared with me her love of movies. She took me to ball practice and listened to my dreams.

We lived in the country and were surrounded by farmer's fields, cows, and woods. Our neighbors were all elderly. My Mammaw lived right next door. The only time I was around kids other than my sister was at church or school. Mom provided the entertainment at home. She was the pitcher in our kickball games, the rebounder when I practiced basketball, and the undisputed champion in Ping-Pong and dodge ball.

My thirteenth birthday came while she was still in the hospital. Pop bought me a birthday cake, but I refused to celebrate until Mom came home. I made them put the cake in the freezer.

I would not come out of my room when I was at home because I did not want to hear what the grown-ups were talking about. I didn't want to face the possibility of losing my mother. During that time, sleep was my escape. I slept so soundly that I didn't disturb the sheets.

The day that Mom came home, I took the cake from the freezer and let it thaw. I told Mom that her being home was the best birthday present that I had ever gotten. Looking back, that was the best cake I ever ate.

Everything that is happening to Benjamin reminds me of when my mother had cancer. I am having so much difficulty dealing with the thought that Benjamin could die that I find myself shutting down.

Looking at Benjamin hold onto Mom's finger makes me realize that the only thing that I have done for these past six weeks is hold onto anything I could — good news from the doctors and nurses — hope. I am afraid to let go because I do not know how far I would fall.

Benjamin is holding on, too. He is holding onto life. He gets his strength from his mother, just like I got strength from mine. It has to be hard on Nicki because not only is she carrying Benjamin, she is carrying me. I recalled today a Bible verse that a friend shared with me a couple of years ago:

> *Trust in the Lord thy God with all thine heart*
> *and lean not unto thine own understanding.*
> **Proverbs 3:5**

That's all I can do. Trust and wait.

APRIL 2

TODAY IS GOOD FRIDAY. Nicki and I began the day by getting vanilla Cokes™ at the *Sonic* drive-in and driving to the hospital. Esther is still our nurse. Benjamin is doing well. He is still puffy from the medicine, but Dr. Wooldridge says that Benjamin's platelet count is coming back up and he is continuing to wean Benjamin from the ventilator.

We ended our visit a little early to catch the 5:30 showing of *The Matrix*. It is one of the best movies I've seen in years. It was so good that my jaw hurt from being clenched for such a long time during the movie.

When we returned to the hospital after dinner, Darrell and Judy were already there. I stayed in the waiting room while Nicki and her mother visited with Benjamin. When I was coming in for the handoff, Nicki met me at the door leading into the scrub room. She usually does this to prep me for something horrible that has happened. She told me that Butch™, Benjamin's faithful Beanie Baby® companion, had taken a hit in the line of fire. Apparently, while Esther was changing him, Benjamin decided to test out his pee shooter by sending a stream of urine toward his face. But Butch™ took the hit. Grandmother Judy agreed to take him home and wash him so that he could return to duty as Benjamin's headpiece.

Nicki bought two books at the mall for me to read to Benjamin — *The Velveteen Rabbit* and a collection of bedtime stories. The first story is one of my all-time favorites — *The Gingerbread Man*.

I love reading the part that says "Run, run, as fast as you can, you can't catch me I'm the Gingerbread Man!" There is something cool about the way that sounds when you say it out loud. That's my biggest gripe with Pokémon™, Barney™, and the Teletubbies™. Nothing they do is cool.

When you think about it, all of today's television shows are designed for merchandising. Nothing about them is creative. Morals have been replaced with marketing. The Gingerbread Man has style.

He is a little cookie that has absolutely nothing going for him — no weapons, no magical powers — he's not even big. He's just a cookie. Still, he has the moxie to taunt everybody in town, daring them to catch him. Sure, the Gingerbread Man has a smart mouth, but that's so you won't feel so bad when the fox eats him.

And it doesn't even matter that hardly anybody in this country knows what a gingerbread man is. I have never seen a gingerbread man. That makes it even better. On the "Fonzie Scale of Cool," The Gingerbread Man gets two thumbs up.

I segued *The Gingerbread Man* into *Goldie Locks and the Three Bears*. While I was reading, I noticed that instead of Mama Bear, Papa Bear, and Baby Bear, it was Mama Bear, Papa Bear, and Little Bear. I found this odd and somewhat worrisome. Why is it Little Bear instead of Baby Bear? Is it because baby bears are cubs? Also, when is porridge to be eaten — for breakfast, lunch, or dinner? The mere fact that we ask these questions is a tribute to the timelessness of this story. Although it makes absolutely no sense in present day times, the story still hits home.

Reading these stories out loud has forced me to reevaluate my parenting skills. Nicki is a great singer/storyteller. She has a lot of energy and inflection in her voice. She also uses choreography. I, on the other hand, lack the ability to read and emphasize my words with punctuation. Commas become periods. God forbid if I have to turn the page. Also, when I try to make eye contact with Benjamin while I am reading, I lose my place.

I have decided that I will practice my story telling so that when Benjamin comes home I will be able to compete with the television and that ubiquitous purple dinosaur.

APRIL 3

NICKI'S AUNT LINDA arrived today from Virginia for a visit. Since she was from out of town, the nurses slipped her in so that she could see Benjamin close up. While Nicki was growing up, Linda and Nicki's grandmother helped raise her. Nicki and Linda are still close.

I met Nicki, Linda, and Judy for lunch that afternoon and got the play-by-play of their visit. Linda told me she had not felt the presence of her mother, Nicki's grandmother, since she passed away until she walked into the hospital to see Benjamin. She sensed Nicki's grandmother was right there beside Benjamin's crib.

Nicki's grandmother raised eight children and countless grandchildren. She lost her sight when Nicki was a child, so Nicki became her eyes. All of Nicki's family revered her because she had the ability to make you feel special. While she was growing up, Nicki would lie in bed with her and listen to the Whippoorwills. The two of them would softly mimic the Whippoorwill's call.

When Nicki was still a little girl, five or six years old, her grandmother wanted to cook. She had not yet adjusted to her blindness, and her children had refused to allow her in the kitchen. Showing the same "rules-are-made-to-be-broken" spirit that my wife now possesses, she simply waited for her children to leave the house so that she could convince a five year old that cooking was a good thing. The two of them went in the kitchen with a "cook-or-be-damned" attitude that made fixing spaghetti an event.

The two of them — an elderly blind woman and a five year old — boiled water, browned meat, chopped vegetables, and ultimately made dinner. In the way the story has been told to me, no mention was made about the quality of the meal because that was not important. What mattered was that the two of them could cook.

Nicki's grandmother would have made a good Marine because she knew how to adapt. If something is taken away — compensate. She may have lost her sight, but she had the boundless courage and able assistance of a grandchild who didn't know that not being able to see was supposed to be a handicap.

I wish this woman had lived long enough for me to meet her and thank her for making my wife the woman that she is today. A lot of Nicki's strength comes from her grandmother. I regret that I have had to learn about her from stories.

That afternoon, the four of us went back to the hospital. Donna was our nurse. She was the nurse on the day that

Benjamin became so sick. As we were talking, Donna confirmed how close Benjamin came to dying that Saturday, March 6.

Just hearing her talk about it rattled me all over again. I knew Benjamin had been close to death because the doctors had prepared us for the chance that he might die, but hearing about it from Donna sent chills up my back. I had to choke back tears. Even though it has been only three weeks ago that all this happened, I tried to pretend that I had just imagined it and that Benjamin was fine.

It has to be hard to be a neonatologist or nurse in an NICU nursery. You are responsible for protecting parents' hopes and dreams. You cannot allow yourself to get too close to the parents, or the babies, because it could damage your objectivity.

One of the difficulties is that the staff is with a family for a long time. We have now been in the hospital for almost two months. We see the doctors and nurses on a daily basis and spend eight to ten hours a day sitting right next to them with nothing to do but talk.

As shy as I sometimes am, I have grown friendly with some of these people. I can see that Esther, Nancy, and Lisa love Nicki and Benjamin. Not only do they love us, they have become our friends.

Tonight, Dr. Buchheit came by and asked us if we were ready for some good news. Benjamin's platelet count was up to 115,000 — the highest it has been since he became sick. Nicki threw both of her arms into the air and then around Dr. Buchheit. As stoic as he has been, he returned the hug, although it was the rigid little double pat that is often practiced by people who are trying to keep their emotions in check.

Dr. Buchheit reminds me of Spock from *Star Trek*. He presents a professional, logical exterior even when he has human emotions. He would never pump his fist in the air and say "You the man," as he read Benjamin's test results. I wish he would. Now that we have gotten to know each other, we get along just fine.

I have noticed that Benjamin does much better when Nicki has her hand on him, soothing him. He is obviously starting to get uncomfortable. A nurse told us that this is a good sign because it is Benjamin's way of telling us that he is ready for the tube to come out of his mouth and begin making real progress. The doctors have started to put water into his stomach to try to jump-start his digestive system.

I can't even imagine what it must be like to immediately bring a baby home from the hospital. We have accepted the fact that Benjamin is on a respirator and that, for him, progress is measured by turning the ventilator down, not coming home. Although the forward steps are small, they are becoming steady. This makes it even more frustrating. We are ready to move forward, but are remaining guarded about getting our hopes up.

When Nicki's grandmother lost her sight, she had to decide how the rest of her life would be spent. She could either withdraw or adjust. Instead of becoming a prisoner in her home, she used the loss of her sight to expand the relationships she had with her family, particularly her grandchildren. She used her reliance upon them to strengthen their relationships.

I think that experience has helped prepare Nicki for the curve ball that we were thrown with Benjamin. Instead of withdrawing and focusing on what we don't have, she has used this as an opportunity to ready herself for what Benjamin needs which is her sitting by his bed with her hand placed lightly on his chest and shoulders while she gently soothes him. This is just as important a skill as if he were home and she were rocking him at bedtime. Although the circumstances are different, he still needs his mother and she still needs to be needed by her son. Watching the two of them adapt so effortlessly brings a sense of peace and purpose to all that we have been through.

The lessons that Nicki learned from her grandmother when she made the adjustment from sight to darkness are being relived today in this nursery. I think Linda is right. I, too, feel the presence of Nicki's grandmother with Benjamin.

APRIL 4

WHEN WE GOT TO THE HOSPITAL this morning, Nurse Esther told us that she had given Benjamin a rectal rocket — the medical term for a suppository.

His platelets are still up and he tolerated his first feeding since becoming sick.

During the evening visit, Nicki got to administer his feeding. The food was still being delivered through a tube, but the nurses let her draw the formula and place it into his feeding tube. We were told that Benjamin would be aware of the sensation that the formula made when it entered his stomach, just like when a baby eats normally.

During the feeding, as if on cue, Benjamin opened his eyes. This is the first time we have seen his eyes open in more than a week. As has every other small step forward, this one was commemorated with multiple pictures.

As he blinked away the sleep, he rolled his head over toward me and our eyes met. I can feel the recognition. It's the first sense I have had that he is aware that I am his father.

His eyes are tired — and he looks horrible. His skin is flaked and dry and his hair is matted. But as he focuses on my face, I feel that we are connecting. I feel that he wants to tell me that he is aware of what is going on and that he is going to be OK. Suddenly, I realize I am crying.

I love him almost more than I can stand. I love him more than I can say in words — more than I can express. I have never known this type of love before. I don't know what I'm supposed to do.

I want to buy him things, I want to hold him, I want to tell him why he is so special, and I want to do all of these things at once. I want to be the one lying in a bed with the tube in my throat — my food lifted above me so that gravity will push it into my stomach. I want to be the one stuck every hour with a needle — on my feet and in my head. I want to be the one forced to lie on my back for six weeks — unable to be moved, unable to be held, and in a room where the lights never go completely out and it never gets quiet.

I want it to be my intestines that don't work and my brain that bleeds. I want to be the one that is sick. I want to suffer all of these things so he won't have to. I look into his eyes and wish that I could take on his suffering, but I don't want him to be in my place. I don't want Benjamin to ever have to worry about what it would be like to lose a child. It is hard for me to go home with Nicki every night and watch her fall asleep in the car because she is so tired — to watch her undress and convince herself in the mirror that she needs to be strong.

I don't want him to be afraid to talk to friends and family — afraid when the telephone rings — afraid when anything happens that is not supposed to happen. I don't want him to feel the fatigue that cannot be cured by rest or feel the frustration of having to spend every day watching instead of doing. I don't wish any of this on my child.

I don't know what else to do but pray. I don't bow my head because I don't want to look away from his beautiful eyes. I don't say anything out loud because I don't want to draw attention to what I am doing. I don't reach out to him because I don't want to disturb the moment being shared by Nicki and the nurse because he opened his eyes during the feeding. I just sit and I pray. My prayer is one of thankfulness and one for strength — for him and for me. I pray for today and for tomorrow. I think this must be what it means to be a father.

APRIL 5

I WENT TO COURT TODAY for the first time since Benjamin was born. It was just a motion that I was handling for Sal, but I was so worked up about it that I wasn't able to sleep last night, worrying about how I would do.

Chancellor Lantrip was the judge. When Terry, the Judge's secretary, saw me in the courthouse, she took me to his office so she and the Judge could ask about Benjamin. They, like most of the people in the courthouse, have been keeping up with Benjamin's progress through Sal, Pratt, and Keith, my partners, and Judy Bates, my office manager. Judy knows all our friends and has been keeping everyone informed. She serves as our spokesperson. Judy is also my unofficial "big sister." In the past, her telephone number has been the only one I could remember in an emergency. So when Terry saw me, she took me to the Judge's office so they would not miss an opportunity to get information firsthand.

I practice in a very specialized field — litigation. I have little client interaction and spend the majority of my time with my cases, preparing them to go to court. As a result, most of the attorneys I get to know are also litigators.

Trial work is difficult. There are no compromises. Someone will win and someone will lose. As a result, the client's stress levels are high and I have the added pressure of making an effective presentation before a judge or jury. My success is measured by victories, not by my performance.

Since all of this started in February, I have found my attention span to be almost zero. I'm oversensitive and I overreact. Those qualities can be deadly for a litigator.

My confidence level is also almost zero. I have been so nervous about getting back to court that I wonder if it will carry over into the rest of my professional life. I was pleased once the hearing began. I was able to not only do it, but to do it well. It was another small victory.

Any good feelings that I had about returning to the courtroom were offset when I got back to my office and received an EOB (explanation of benefits) from my insurance carrier indicating that they were not going to pay for Benjamin's medical bills because he was not covered as a dependant. To date, the bill for Benjamin's medical expenses is well over $250,000. When I received the denial letter from my carrier, I had no idea how I was going to pay for his care.

Thankfully, the EOB was just a billing glitch. Benjamin had not yet been added on in the system as a dependent. I know that it is bad to think about insurance at a time like this, and I

EQUAL TO THE TASK

FEBRUARY 28
Benjamin is wearing baby "shades." He needs ultraviolet light to treat jaundice.

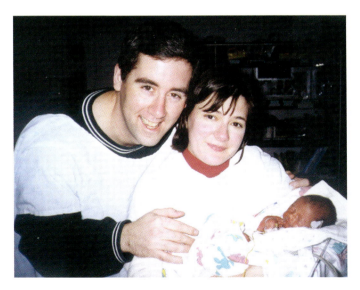

FEBRUARY 28
Dail, Nicki, and Benjamin. The first family picture.

DAIL CANTRELL

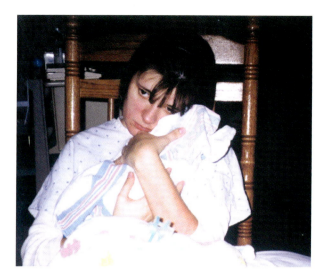

MARCH 4
Nicki's expression says it all – Benjamin is not doing well.

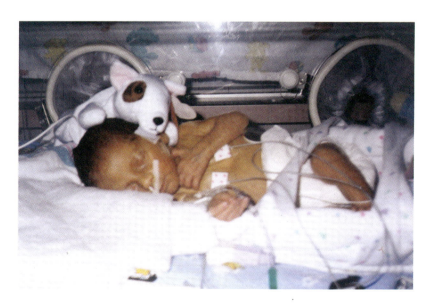

MARCH 4
Picture taken four hours before Benjamin went on full life support.

EQUAL TO THE TASK

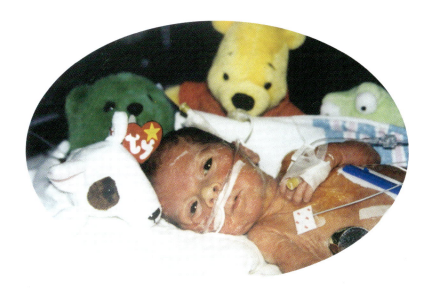

MARCH 17
Benjamin and Beanie Baby® Butch™. Benjamin is well enough today to come off the respirator.

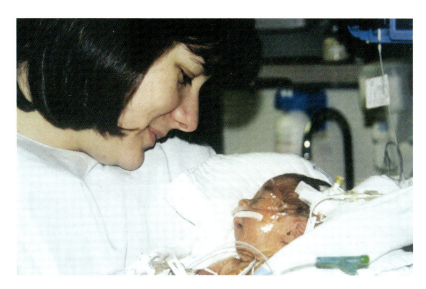

MARCH 17
Finally Nicki can hold Benjamin again.

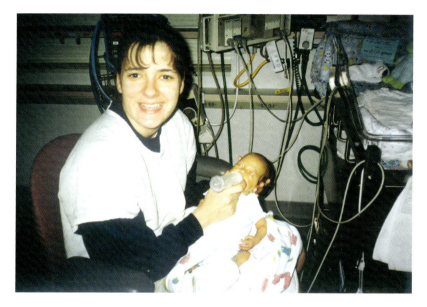

APRIL 15
The first step toward home — Benjamin's first bottle!

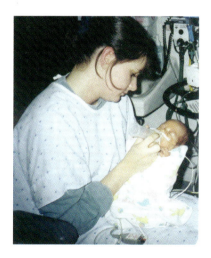

APRIL 17
Another step toward home —
full-strength formula.

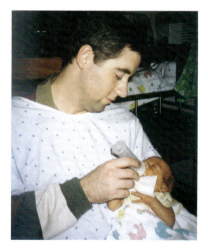

APRIL 19
Dail takes a turn feeding
Benjamin.

EQUAL TO THE TASK

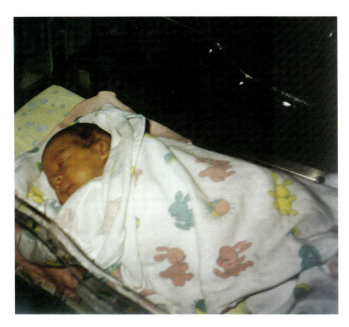

STAGE II: Benjamin is big enough to sleep in a bassinet.

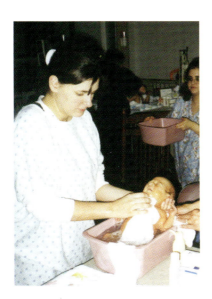

STAGE II: Benjamin's hot tub.

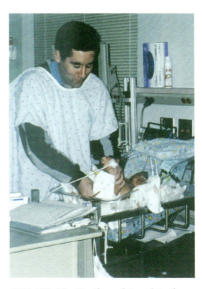

STAGE II: Dail making his first solo diaper change.

DAIL CANTRELL

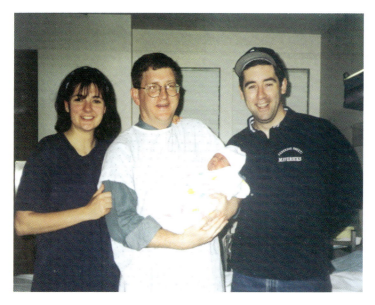

A P R I L   3 0
Another step toward home — discharge instructions from Dr. Buchheit.

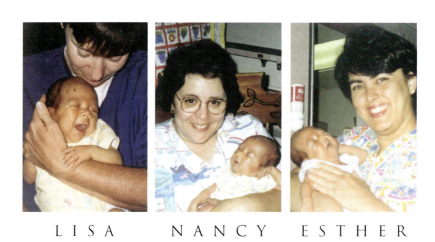

L I S A   N A N C Y   E S T H E R

NICU nurses work around the clock, constantly observing the baby. In Stage I, they never leave the baby's bedside even when the parents are there.

EQUAL TO THE TASK

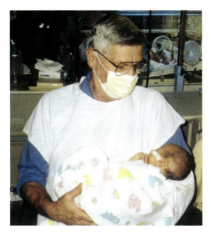

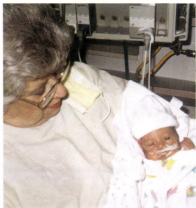

POP   MOM

Papaw Bill finally held Benjamin, but he would not give up the protective mask, even though everyone else had. Memaw Sarah is looking for a family resemblance.

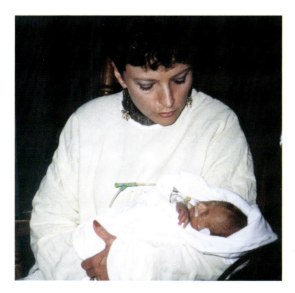

JUDY

Grandma Judy and Benjamin in the rocking chair. A benefit of being in Stage II is being able to pick up your baby any time.

DAIL CANTRELL

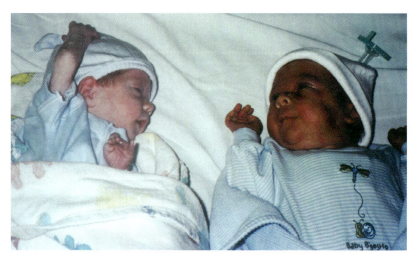

COULTER AND BENJAMIN
APRIL 30

These two friends are finally able to see each other up close for the first time. Coulter is two days older than Benjamin. Both boys were able to go home on the same day. They are still friends and see each other regularly.

APRIL 30
A very excited Nicki. Judy and the "miracle baby."

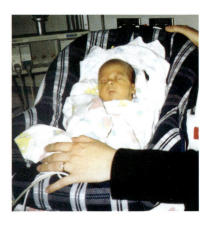

APRIL 30
Going home — Benjamin's first ride in a car seat.

would have made any arrangements possible to pay for his care, but it seemed like just one more burden to carry.

At lunch I went to visit Matt. While I was at his office, I met a couple in the waiting room that I had read about in the local newspaper. The husband had donated a kidney to his wife who was has polycystic fibrosis, the same disease that Nicki has. The article about them was in the newspaper because it is rare that one spouse is able to donate a kidney to the other spouse.

The couple has a child who contracted spinal meningitis when he was six years old. Brain damage resulting from the illness has caused him to be autistic. They shared several stories with me about their struggles. Although I appreciated their effort, it scared me.

One of the things that Nicki and I don't talk about is the potential for long-term developmental problems that Benjamin might have, such as autism, cerebral palsy, and other brain-related defects. Although I am hopeful that Benjamin will not suffer any of these complications, the threat hangs over me, dragging me down. The uncertainty that comes from not knowing is really wearing on me. I am thankful that he has come through everything, but I am fearful of what lies ahead.

Nicki has been a tower of strength, not focusing on tomorrow, but just on today. I am consumed by the thought of tomorrow. I am consumed by doubt and I am consumed by fear. I have tried to focus on the next hospital visit, but the apprehension of walking back to his crib, of bracing myself for whatever bad news is to be delivered, is devastating.

Nicki called me today at lunchtime with some good news. Benjamin's platelet count has risen to 130,000, which was almost to the normal range, and he is tolerating his feedings. The problem is that he is not having any bowel movements.

I met Nicki for dinner and when we went back for the evening visit, Lisa was our nurse. She gave us some great news — Benjamin had a poop and he kept most of his feeding down. Nicki was so excited that she hugged Lisa — twice.

Tonight I read Benjamin the story about *The Three Billy Goats Gruff*. I didn't remember this story being as violent as it is. It is an ancient Scandinavian fairy tale about killing a troll that lives under the bridge. I was stunned. Tipper Gore should be checking out some of these fairy tale books and lay off the movie and music industry. If I were a five year old and someone told me this story, I would be terrified every time I saw a goat. Goats are scary enough, with those horns and the butting, but the thought that they would kill things makes them demonic. I can see now why kids have nightmares when they read stories like this one and *The Gingerbread Man*. The characters always meet with a violent death.

During my visit, I watched the parents of the baby next to us get to hold her for the first time. She is their third child. This is apparent by the confidence they showed when passing the baby back and forth between them. I have not yet been brave enough to pick Benjamin up, let alone pass him off.

Watching the two of them take turns holding their baby, while the other one snapped pictures, made me think about how I don't really take the time to appreciate the simple things in life. With me it has always been about planning and execution, not appreciation. My trial calendar is prepared almost two years I advance. Each day is divided into fifteen-minute segments. If I want to take a vacation, I have to start thinking about scheduling over a year in advance.

Being at the hospital everyday has put me almost six months behind in my work. Before Benjamin was born, I worked every Saturday and almost every night until 6:30. Now I have just stopped. The only place I want to be is with him. I find that I am watching everything a little closer and things that I have always taken for granted, such as holding a child, now have new meaning.

While I am looking around, I can't help but think about Baby Brandon. He seems to have taken a turn for the worse. If there is another child that I am praying for as much as Benjamin, it has to be this little boy. The nurses have begun covering him because he is so swollen and disfigured. His mother and father are two of the most pleasant people in the nursery. They are always upbeat and are genuinely loved by the nursing staff.

Looking at them gives me confidence, yet it also causes despair. I pray that Brandon will get to go home and grow up and be a healthy young man. One day I will find him and tell him how much all of us were rooting for him.

Baby Coulter is going to have to have surgery for reflux. If he handles that surgery well, there will be another surgery in a week to ten days to put a shunt into his head. I pray for Coulter, too.

Benjamin had another cranial ultrasound today, but I won't know the results until tomorrow — another day of waiting.

One of my prayers is that through all of this I will become a better person. I hope that Benjamin's trials and tribulations have not been some sort of punishment for the sins and transgressions that I have committed throughout my life. I have to trust that God is a kind and loving God. I deliver Benjamin unto him.

A P R I L 6

"SORRY, WE HAVE A NEW BABY." As a parent of a child in the NICU, I dread hearing those words because whenever a new baby is brought into the NICU, I know it will take approximately two hours to set up the intensive care isolette.

The way the nursery is set up, all new arrivals are put in critical care isolettes. The doctors and nurses spend the two hours getting everything set up and stabilizing the baby. While this is going on, no visitors are allowed in this section of the nursery. The hospital obviously cannot control what time babies come so if it happens near the beginning of visiting hours, parents and grandparents have to wait in the lounge. Tonight that means it would be after ten o'clock before we even get to see Benjamin.

Children's Hospital does not have a place for babies to be delivered. So in Nicki's case, when there were complications with her pregnancy, we were transferred from our home hospital to a critical care specialist located at Fort Sanders Hospital which is located directly across the street from Children's Hospital. This would allow Benjamin to be transported directly to Children's Hospital via the underground tunnel that connects the two hospitals.

Children's Hospital accepts babies from all across the region. Our particular hospital is located in Knoxville, Tennessee and it services the entire eastern section of the state to the Cumberland Plateau. Babies are also accepted from Alabama, northern Georgia, Kentucky, and southwest Virginia.

Children's Hospital has a special ambulance which is used to transport newborns. It is about twice the size of a regular ambulance. A neonatologist and a transport team of nurses travel to the hospital where the baby has been born and pick up the new arrival.

The NICU is only for newborns. Once a baby leaves the hospital, it cannot come into the neonatal unit. These babies are admitted to a separate nursery. The transport team of doctor and nurses is trained and equipped to handle any emergency that might arise.

The survival rate of children that actually make it to the NICU is nearly 98%. This NICU handles over 600 babies each year. The greatest difficulty the doctors and nurses face is getting the baby from the birth hospital to Children's Hospital.

The special ambulance is equipped to travel between two and half and three hours away. Anything farther than that becomes a problem. I suppose it would be possible to have helicopter transport because I have seen a helipad on top of the hospital. Since we have been at Children's Hospital, I have not heard any of the doctors or nurses talk about using the helicopter, but it would not surprise me to learn that this service is also available. The transport team includes an experienced nurse and someone who can operate a portable ventilator. Three to four people usually assist the doctor during transport.

The number one reason for admission into the NICU is premature birth. There are a host of health complications that are associated with a premature delivery. Girls mature quicker than boys do and Caucasian males are weaker than non-Caucasians. This condition is sometimes called "wimpy white boy syndrome." These statistics were played out in the NICU. While Benjamin has been a patient, over 90% of his nursery mates have been white males.

From talking with the nurses, the danger zone for boys is birth earlier than 28 weeks, preferably they should be 30 to32 weeks. Girls mature about two weeks earlier.

The smallest baby that I have seen in the NICU is a girl. She is from Crossville, Tennessee and was delivered at 25 weeks. She barely weighed a pound. She has been in the NICU for almost a month and has not developed any health complications. She was recently been moved to the feeder-grower side and apparently will go home in another four to six weeks.

She was so small when she was born that her skin had yet to develop. It was translucent. The nurses had stretched cellophane across her crib to provide extra humidity and warmth and decrease the possibility of stimulation caused by air passing over her crib. When the nurses needed to stimulate her because of an A&B spell, they ripped the cellophane away and gently jostled her from side to side. Once her A& B spell subsided, they wrapped her isolette in cellophane again.

A&B's are common throughout the nursery. A&B stands for apnea and bradycardia, which means that the baby quits breathing or its heart slows. This is a common occurrence in preemies. When an A&B spell occurs, you merely stimulate the child. This can be as simple as a gentle shake or a light pinch to restart the baby's breathing and heartbeat.

When an A&B spell occurs, the monitor makes a small sound. These monitors go off continually throughout the nursery. Over time, I have started to drown them out. The first time an A&B occurred when I was holding Benjamin, our nurse looked up and told me to stimulate him. As I gently tried to rouse him, this was met with a chuckle from everybody around me. Nancy, one of the nurses that I had befriended, reached from behind me and gave Benjamin a solid jostle. This started him breathing again and made the monitors go off. I was instructed that Benjamin would not break and that I should not hesitate to be more aggressive.

A&B's subside as the child grows. Most premature infants are sent home on a heart monitor. This in itself is somewhat intimidating. A cuff is placed over the baby's hand or foot. During the night, if the baby has an A&B spell, the monitor sounds an alarm so the parents can come and rouse the baby. Most of the time, the monitor is so loud that it will wake the baby and the problem will correct itself.

Benjamin has really not had much of a problem with A&B spells. His two major areas of concern are the intraventricular hemorrhages and the NEC that affected his bowel. Baby Coulter had surgery today for reflux, another common problem with premature babies. Coulter is still scheduled to have a shunt implanted in about a week to ten days. The shunt will last his entire lifetime and it is designed to grow with him. This allows the fluid to drain from his cranial cavity.

Our primary concern with Benjamin right now is that he is still not having bowel movements. There is a lot of gas and excess waste in his system, causing him to bloat and have a lot of discomfort. He is tolerating his feedings, but the fact that he is having no bowel movements is a concern.

Esther has been our nurse today. When Nicki called to check on Benjamin before driving in, Esther told her to be prepared for how bloated he looked. After Nicki dressed, she went in when visiting hours began and met with the surgeon, who still does not want to operate.

Due to the admission of the new baby, we did not finish our evening visit until almost two in the morning. That meant that it would be almost four before I got home and went to bed.

THE LONG WAY HOME

On the way home, Nicki made the comment that the oldies rock station that we were listening to played essentially the same songs every day. This particular station only seems to know *Maggie May* by Rod Stewart, *Hotel California* by the Eagles, and *Slow Ride* by Fog Hat. A recent addition is *Pinball Wizard* by The Who. Given that Nicki is a decade younger than I am, she considers the rock standards that I grew up with to be oldies. She has absolutely no appreciation for these groups or their music. I tried to educate her by giving her a little background about the song and the group. Every time a band other than the Beatles came on, I would ask her, "Who is singing?" Her standard answer is now The Who. It does not matter if it is The Kinks, Crosby, Stills and Nash, or The Rolling Stones. If it is a group, Nicki thinks it is The Who.

As we were leaving the hospital tonight, Nicki said that she thought she heard Benjamin toot. I was too blurry eyed to make any confirmation, but Nurse Lisa said she thought she heard it as well. When she said this, Nicki hugged her. Lisa shyly said that she didn't have to be hugged for toots — just for poops. Life's little wonders.

APRIL 7

TONIGHT I READ BENJAMIN THE STORY of the *Tortoise and the Hare*. I told him that he was the tortoise. Although it may not look like he will win the race right now, if he keeps on running, everything will be OK.

Fatigue has become my constant companion. We usually leave the hospital between one and two in the morning and by the time we drive home and get settled in, it is nearly four in the morning. I try to get to work around 8:30 each morning, which means that I'm operating on between three and four hours of sleep. Nicki leaves to go to the hospital when I go to work. I try to arrange for one of my friends to drive me to the hospital around 4:30 to 5:00 so that I can drive her home in the evening.

The nurses have developed a routine. Now that we have been here for nearly two months, it is obvious that certain nurses have requested to be assigned to Benjamin. This serves two purposes. First, it allows for a continuity of care. The nurse becomes familiar with Benjamin's habits and therefore can be a better caregiver. Second, the families become comfortable with the nurses.

In our case, we have three primary nurses — Esther in the morning and Nancy and Lisa in the evening. These nurses are three of the more experienced nurses on the floor and have been a blessing for us.

Esther and Nicki have formed a special bond. Nicki spends the majority of the day by herself, except when the grandparents come by for a visit. I have grown particularly close with the evening nurses, Lisa and Nancy. They kid with me and have turned visits into fun time.

This evening Lisa brought out Benjamin's bathtub, which is a big plastic basin that has "Ben's Hot Tub" written on the side. Nicki got to give him a bath pretty much unassisted. While she was bathing him, his eyes opened. They flicker like firelight. It's times like this when I begin to feel like a father, even though I didn't do anything during the bath but watch. I felt such pride watching my wife and son.

I think that is what the nurses do best. They help me feel like a parent.

Nicki and I feel so helpless. Although we only live a little over thirty minutes from the hospital, it seems so far away. I don't know how parents who live two or three hours away can stand it. Life has to continue. We still have to work. We still have to go on with our lives. Just because our child is in the hospital, everything else doesn't stop. Thankfully, we have no other children at home. Benjamin has been in the NICU for almost eight weeks. I have gone back to work, but Nicki stays with him about

15 to 17 hours a day. During this time, there is little for us to do but sit and look at him. We can't hold him — we can't change him — we can't do anything for him without the assistance of the nurses.

The nurses have started including us in the care-giving process. Lisa and Esther have given Nicki the responsibility of bathing Benjamin and putting moisturizer on his skin where it is so flaked and chapped. Nancy has one of us hold him while the other one helps to change his bed. They also make sure that whenever we are present and it is time to do a feeding that we hold the syringe up high to let the formula spill into his stomach. Although this does not seem like much, it is important for us to feel that we are caregivers.

Nicki lives for the times when she gets to be a mother. I yearn for the time that I can be a father. I have never changed a diaper. I have never made formula. The only other baby that I remember holding is my nephew and that felt awkward. One day Benjamin will be coming home and Nicki and I will be responsible for his life. When I stand at his crib and see him hooked up to all of the machines, everything seems so foreign. The reality is that in the coming months there will be times when I will be alone with him at our home, away from the hospital, away from the doctors and nurses, and I will be the one to feed him and clean him up. It will be my responsibility to see that he sleeps and that he is protected. The nurses are helping prepare us for that time.

When Benjamin was so sick, the natural tendency was to become hesitant with him. Although he is approaching two months old, he has still not yet reached his due date. The nurses are careful that Nicki and I don't think of him as so fragile that we forget how to love him. They are not only caregivers — they are teachers.

In the race to become parents, Nicki and I are also tortoises. As I wait for sleep to come, to get me to tomorrow, I focus on the fact that the race is not won by the fastest, but the strongest. I must be strong.

APRIL 8

WHEN WE GOT HOME TONIGHT, I thought I was having a heart attack. It felt like someone was jabbing a knife into the center of my chest. The pain was so intense it made me double over and fall on the floor. I couldn't catch my breath. I couldn't straighten out. It lasted for almost fifteen minutes. But I know my heart is fine. This is just another of the increasing number of stress attacks I am having.

As a litigator and a coach, I am accustomed to stress and I have always been able to cope with it. I feel that the performance of an athlete is enhanced by stress. However, nothing has prepared me for what it is like to have a child in the NICU. The constant roller coaster of emotions, combined with the fatigue and the stress, is beginning to show.

During the morning I was with a client when one of my secretaries interrupted me to tell me that Nicki was on the telephone. Panic washed over me and I became dizzy as I excused myself to take the call. I immediately thought the worst and prepared myself for the worst, unable to separate good from bad.

The news turned out to be positive. The doctors had increased the amount of his feedings and the strength of the mixture, decreasing the amount of the water diluting his formula. He has still not had a bowel movement, but the doctors are hopeful that his excretory system will kick in soon and they will not have to do surgery.

When I arrived for a late afternoon visit, I thought Benjamin looked worse — not that gray, khaki color he had when he was so sick, but bloated and tired. He is retaining so much fluid and gas that it distorts the features of his face. He is so puffy that his eyes are swollen shut.

During our evening visit, he couldn't open his eyes and he rarely moved. The nurses told us this is to be expected because his body was trying to kick-start itself. In fact, the doctor has turned his ventilator down to 14. This meant that in every minute, it was only breathing for him 14 times. The rest he was doing on his own.

As I walked to Benjamin's crib for my evening visit, I noticed that Baby Brandon was no longer in his isolette. As long as we have been in the nursery, he has occupied the same space

— second from the end on the left-hand side facing the window. When I saw that he was not there, I feared that he had died.

I cornered Nancy and asked her what had happened. The nurses are extremely protective about the privacy of the families and will never give any details about the other babies. I have been praying so hard for this baby that I did not want to confront the fact that he could be dead.

Nancy told me that he had been moved to the back corner in an isolation room. Although she did not tell me the reason, I can only assume that it is because he looks so bad. His stomach is so bloated it's hard to believe he is a child. It is almost ten times normal size. He can't be doing well. To give him some dignity and his parents some privacy, the nurses have moved him away from the fishbowl that is created around the observation window.

Tonight I read Benjamin the story of *The Frog Prince*. I find it somewhat ironic that, in theory, Benjamin, Brandon, and Coulter are frogs. They are all sick and they don't look like normal babies. Deep inside though, I know that all three are princes and that as they grow up they will be strong and gentle men.

It is impossible to compare our children to other babies. They are not handicapped — they are not disadvantaged — they are merely sick. When they get better they will be who they are supposed to be. Just because they look different now, doesn't mean they will be sick forever.

In many ways I am still a frog. When I kiss Benjamin goodbye, I wonder what he, Brandon, and Coulter will become some day. I am going to remember this moment in their lives so that I can share it with their families and their children. I can't wait to tell their babies how Daddy, for a short time, was a prince trapped in a frog's body.

But even as I think these thoughts, I know that they are not true. In my eyes and in Nicki's eyes, Benjamin is the most beautiful baby in the world. We would not trade him for anything — just like Brandon and Coulter's parents would not trade their sons for anything. They are already princes.

APRIL 9

BENJAMIN HAD A BOWEL MOVEMENT — not a tiny spot of poop, but a full-sized stinky bowel movement! Nicki called from the hospital to tell me. In the solitude of my office, I threw my hands in the air and ran around the room.

Today Benjamin had his first eye exam. A potential complication with babies who receive oxygen for an extended period of time is that they have a tendency to have retinal damage to their eyes. The eye doctor did an exam and told us that we would know the results by evening.

...le to see. As it turned out, my fears were unfounded, but I ...n't help but worry.

I cannot imagine how difficult the process would be with...he support of our friends and family. My Mom and Pop ...Nicki's mother, dad, and stepfather have been at the hospi...veryday. Just the fact that they are here, reassuring us that ...day everything is going to be OK and sharing in each little ... step forward, has been like a tonic.

The people at the office have carried me. Someone from ...office takes me to the hospital every day. The women treat ...like their son or brother and not the boss. The little words of ...ouragement from Pam, Carla, Marita, Judy, and Jayme carry ... through the day. The attorneys I work with, Pratt, Sal, and ...th, take me to lunch and help take my mind off of the ...blems.

The other attorneys in town and judges have rearranged ... dockets and their calendars to fit my schedule. A lawyer in ...oxville, whose nickname is Snake and who has a reputation ... being a bare-knuckled litigator, has several cases with me. ...en he found out that Benjamin was so ill, he took the lead in ...cheduling depositions and getting new trial dates. It is this ...ntlemanly type of conduct by other members of the bar and ...e bench that make me proud to be lawyer.

I hate lawyer jokes. To me, they are just as derogatory as ...cist jokes. People that make them don't know the fine men ...d women that fill these roles. I can honestly say that the ...ajority of the attorneys and judges that I deal with are some of ...e most honorable people that I have ever encountered.

When we arrived for the evening v
nurse and Lisa was right next door. The tw
only friends that worked together can do. I l
able four-hour visit ever.

The eye screening came back good an(
been turned down to 8. I joked with Nancy
was going to change the sign that explained al
of premature babies, apnea and bradycardia,
ter C for the constant pressure of being paren
NICU. Each victory is weighed against po
Although Benjamin was beginning to make r(
obstacles that I never knew existed would arise

If I had been asked last night if I were (
Benjamin's eyesight, I would have said no. Non
or nurses had ever given any indication that we
cerned about blindness. It was not until the eye
up do the screening that we realized this was an(

The logic behind their reasoning is obvious
need to worry parents about something they
Benjamin had to have oxygen to stay alive — ther(
be on the ventilator. There is no discussion as to w
we can leave him on the ventilator because he wo
out it. Therefore, there is no need to advise parents
tial side effect of long-term dependence on oxygen
What would we do — turn it off?

Therefore, it is things like this that make th(
trying. Ever since Nicki told me about the eye test,
worrying for eight hours about whether or not Benja

Although I do not know them on a personal level, when they found out about Benjamin, I did not need to ask for their help because it was freely given. If I am ever put in a position to help another attorney, particularly a young one, that will be how I thank these people who have helped me throughout the years.

I think about how my sister and her husband have become parents. They are close to my age and have done an incredible job raising Adam. They love their new nephew Benjamin as if he were their own. So do our friends.

Nicki's best friend Jenny has now made the stop at Children's Hospital a part of her daily routine on the way home from school. Our friends frequently take us to dinner. If something needs to be done, they do it.

It is this support that has made the process bearable. The people who protect us, therefore protect him.

The love and affection of these caregivers have eased the memory of the pressure cooker that has described my life for the past two months. I am forever in their debt.

APRIL 10

I LOVE SLEEPING LATE — not just a few hours, but making a day of it. Today was Saturday and I didn't get up until after 11:00 this morning. It was wonderful!

I hear parents talk all the time about making sure their kids were in bed by 7:30 or 8:00 so that they get enough rest. I have decided that I'm going to let Benjamin stay up as late as he wants. If he wants to stay up until 2:00, that's fine — as long as he gets up for school the next morning. I figure that he will regulate himself and learn how much sleep he needs.

When I was little, my father worked shift work. Every other week he worked from 3:00 in the afternoon until 11:00 at night. When I was in school that meant I only got to see him in the morning and at night when he got home.

My sister always went to bed early — no one had to tell her — she was usually in bed by 9:00. I was a night owl. I stayed up and watched Johnny Carson and waited for Pop to arrive home about a quarter before twelve. That was usually enough time to get through Johnny's monologue and the *Mighty Carson Art Players*.

I would wait for Pop to get home. As soon as he walked in, I would hug Pop and he would carry me on his back to the bedroom. These late nights are among my favorite childhood memories.

After Ann went go to bed, Mom and I would watch television. When I was growing up, there was no such thing as cable. We only got two of the three network channels, NBC and CBS. Therefore, our options at night were pretty limited. Johnny Carson was our favorite.

I think I learned more from *The Johnny Carson Show* and Mom explaining the jokes in his monologue than I did from school. We had an old six-cushion couch that sat against the wall across from the television. Mom and I would get a blanket and she would sit on one end while I sat on the other. And every night we would watch Johnny Carson.

When Pop got home, he would make a big production out of carrying me to bed. I used to get to sleep in his and Mom's bed until I went to sleep. Then he would move me to my bed. That ended when I was about five years old and got hold of Mom's perfume spray. I had seen the cartoons where Peppy Le Pue, the skunk, would squeeze the big ball and make a big cloud. I knew that Mom had one of these devices so I sprayed perfume on everything — the sheets, the pillows, Dad's clothes, anything that I could get hold of. That was the end of sleeping in my parents' bed.

I have already decided that I am going to carry Benjamin to bed on my shoulders every night. Thankfully, I work in a job where I will be home in the evenings, but I am going to let him stay up as late as he wants to and every night when he goes to bed I am going to carry him.

I am going to sit with him on the couch and explain the television shows to him and answer all of his questions just like my mom answered all of mine. This is going to be my contribution as a parent.

We have settled into a routine at the hospital that involves sitting and watching Benjamin for the majority of the day. Since he is making slow and steady improvement, I have a lot more time to observe the other parents. The father of the baby across from Benjamin is a nurse. His baby apparently is not doing well. I watched this baby's mother sing and comfort him much the same way that I sang to Benjamin seven weeks ago. The father is being difficult because he wants things done fast. I was so scared when Benjamin got sick that I didn't even know what to ask for. This dad wants blood transfusions and demands to see the doctors. That makes the nurses much more cautious around him. I want to take him aside and tell him to trust them — they do a great job. I can tell he is a concerned father who loves his son. It is frustrating for him not to be able to do more.

I want to tell all of the parents to trust the doctors and the nurses. Nancy is our nurse again this evening, and she continues my parent education. I have gotten so comfortable with her that I now spend four to five hours grilling her with questions. I ask questions about everything. What can I expect when we get home? Will Benjamin have any long-term effects from his illness? I ask everything I can think of. She just laughs and answers my questions and calms me down.

Nicki noticed that Benjamin was having some skin chaffing around his testicles and pointed this out to the nurses. I am amazed at how good a mother she has already become so quickly. Her responsibilities grow each day. It is obvious that in our family she will be the one that dispenses the Band-Aids™ and the discipline. I will carry Benjamin to bed and let him watch television. My role will be that of a spiritual advisor.

During our visit, I heard a pecking on the observation window across the room. I looked up and saw it was one of my students from the law school trying to get my attention. He had a question that he wanted to ask about his exam and felt confident enough to take me away from my visit with Benjamin.

I was startled at how brazen he was, but somehow was comforted in that he felt confident enough to pull me away. Surely if Benjamin were going to die, I think, this student would not have interrupted me.

This is the first night that I have ever been able to sit and watch Benjamin and think about what kind of parent I am going to be. I have spent the majority of my time praying that he won't die — that he won't be retarded — that he won't be handicapped. Now I am actually thinking about being a dad. It feels pretty good.

APRIL 11

I FEEL LIKE I AM SICK ALL OF THE TIME. Last night I had another massive anxiety attack. I lay on the floor and held onto my knees for almost ten minutes. It was like my chest was being ripped apart. It hurt so badly I cried.

Nicki made me leave the hospital early to try and get some rest. That was a mistake. Although I got home close to 9:00, all I did was worry about Benjamin and about Nicki. I decided that I would not let myself call and check on them. I settled in to watch the *X Files*, but as soon as it was over, I broke down and called.

Benjamin's ventilator has been cut down from 8 to 4, back up to 8, and then down to 6. I have started to hate the ventilator. It is the only thing preventing Nicki from holding Benjamin.

Before I left the hospital, Benjamin seemed to be doing well. His eyes are open and he is alert, but he is grumpy. The monitor has to be driving him mad. He spit up a little food while I was there and seemed to choke, but the nurses didn't say anything.

His bowel movements are going well. He had six just today — two of them were real big-time poops. The doctors have told us that they don't think he will need to have any surgery for his bowel. It is now just a matter of him getting well enough to come off of the ventilator.

When I sit by his bed and Nancy and Lisa aren't there, I find I can't do anything but watch the monitor. I watch for every change. I watch his ventilator. I watch his heart monitor. I watch everything except Benjamin. I tried to make myself look away, but I am drawn to the monitor. When Nancy and Lisa are there, they take my mind off the monitor and subtly focus my attention back to Benjamin.

When Nicki and I sit with him, I keep my hands to my side. It hurts just to look at him. I hate the frustration on Nicki's face when she places her hand across his chest. I don't know what is worse — the separation or the fatigue. I have become short-tempered, easily distracted, and it's impossible for me to rest or relax. What's even worse is that Nicki is getting on a different schedule. She doesn't go to the hospital until 10:00 or 11:00 which means that she can sleep late. It also means that we are staying at the hospital later into the evening. I don't even consider going home until after 1:00 — its usually 2:00 or 3:00 before we leave — and I am back at work at 8:30 to 9:00 the next morning. I don't know how much longer I can last.

APRIL 12

I HAD MY FIRST BAD EXPERIENCE with a nurse today. It was with a nurse who was fairly new in the NICU. Esther had the day off so we drew someone new as the daytime nurse. Nicki had decided to spend today running errands so we went over to the hospital together at 5:00. This meant that we would have a short visit before dinner and then have our normal evening visit.

When Nicki and I arrived at Benjamin's crib, the nurse immediately became confrontational. When I began looking through Benjamin's daily chart, she asked me what I was doing. I didn't know what to say. This is the first thing I always do.

In fact, one of my favorite things to do when I get to the hospital is to read Benjamin's chart. It calms me down. Rarely do I look at the nurses' notes because they usually do a fairly good job of updating me on the days' events. What I focus on are the doctors' notes. This nurse questioned the fact that I was reading Benjamin's chart. She wanted to know why. When I told her that it was something I did regularly, she came right out and asked me if I was questioning the way she did her job.

I didn't know how to respond and tried to make light of it, explaining that I worked with medical records and I felt comfortable reading a chart. She then responded that every nurse did their records differently and that I wouldn't be able to read her notes. When I tried to change the subject, she walked away in a huff.

While Nicki and I were sitting there, I realized that the rest of the nursery was empty. Unbelievably, we are the only parents visiting at this time. While we were there, the charge nurse buzzed Nicki's mother back, apparently waiving the two-people limit rule. When Judy arrived, our nurse ran back over and demanded that one of us leave. As Judy tried to explain that the charge nurse had sent her in, this nurse went ballistic. She said that it was against the rules and if they bent the rules for one they would have to bend them for all. Considering the fact that my wife and my mother-in-law have much shorter fuses than I do, and were ready to attack, I decided discretion was the better part of valor and volunteered to leave.

About fifteen minutes later, Nicki came out of the nursery crying. I asked her what was wrong and she stated that they had had to manually bag Benjamin when his oxygen stats dropped way down. Apparently what happened was that while he was being fed, he had a large bowel movement. His nurse became concerned about this, not realizing that this was one of our goals. At this point, the nurse overreacted and began fiddling with the oxygen unit, knocking one of the hoses off. A respiratory therapist had to be called in to fix it. Donna, the senior nurse on staff, interceded and told us not to worry that only a hose had been knocked off. Benjamin was fine. His nurse then blamed Nicki for the problem with the hose. This was more than Nicki could stand and she had to leave.

We had dinner with Coulter's parents and told them about our misadventure. Coby, Coulter's mom, suggested that we talk to the head nurse and request a change.

The nursery staff has been so wonderful that I was hesitant to say anything, but I couldn't stand the thought of Nicki having to go back and encounter this nurse again. I shouldn't have worried — as usual, the charge nurse handled the situation wonderfully. She made me feel like one of the family. I felt like I had finally accomplished something. Nicki and I were able to have a great visit and get home early.

APRIL 13

NICKI DRESSED BENJAMIN in a little blue outfit today. This is the first time since he has been in the nursery that he has been able to wear clothes. The nurses and doctors have taken him off the warmer, so we had to dress him to keep him warm.

While Benjamin has been in the nursery, he has been under a device that essentially serves the same function as a heat lamp. Heat comes from above him and his bed is warmed. There have been too many wires and tubes in him to allow us to put clothes on him. The doctors gave us advance warning that they were going to turn off the warmer so Nicki could bring the little blue outfit for him to wear. As you can imagine, this made her feel wonderful. I have always teased Nicki that when Benjamin was born we were only going to dress him in little white T-shirts — that I thought too much money was spent by parents on baby clothes. Of course, we now have received no less than 50 little baby outfits and Benjamin has not yet been able to wear any of them. The fact that Nicki could dress him made me feel like he was really ours.

Although his bowel movements have become more regular, he has thrown up two of his feedings. This might be a sign that he is having a problem with reflux. His oxygen has been taken down so that he is on CPAP, meaning he is receiving no breaths from the ventilator, just help with his own natural breathing. Esther told us this was a huge step toward his coming off the ventilator. I am afraid to get excited because it seems that we are always getting up and then being let down. When Benjamin comes off the ventilator, it means we get to hold him and it will be a huge step toward going home.

Tonight's visit was one of anticipation.

APRIL 14

BENJAMIN CAME OFF THE RESPIRATOR! Nicki called this morning while I was meeting with a client and told me that he had been cut down to CPAP and that if he tolerated his feedings, they might remove the ventilator. She called me back around two that afternoon and said that they were getting ready to take the tube out! I left and rushed to the hospital. But by the time I got there, the tube had been removed and Benjamin was resting peacefully.

Nicki waited until I got there to hold him and hold him she did. As soon as I walked through the door, she ran over and hugged me and then plopped down in the chair for the nurse to hand her the baby.

She held him until visiting time was over — almost two hours. It was wonderful! We didn't talk to each other. The nurses or doctors didn't disturb us. We just sat there together and held our baby.

While I was holding Benjamin, I heard music playing. In the two months that we had been in the NICU, I have never before heard anything but the monitors and people talking. The mother of the baby across from Benjamin had put a tape recorder in his crib that played gospel music. While the music was playing, the nursery became so quiet that I could hear every note. There were no words, just a piano playing hymns.

The tape was not professionally made. It was just a cassette tape of someone playing a piano, probably the baby's mother. What drew my attention was the song — *In the Garden*. This is my favorite hymn.

My Mammaw taught me this hymn. She used to sing it when we were hanging clothes on a line to dry. Mammaw didn't have a clothes dryer. When I was little, she used to get me to help her hang the wet clothes across the old line strung up in her backyard. She had an apron with all of her clothespins in it that I got to wear while she hung up her laundry. She sang *In the Garden* when we hung the clothes on the line, and she sang *Bringing in the Sheaves* when we took them down.

Mammaw lived right next door to me, so I got to see her every day. My favorite thing to play with was the old apron full of clothespins. I would put them on my fingers and my nose and make men out of them. I would stack several of them in a row, and sometimes I would build a pyramid. My favorite time was when she did laundry because that was when Mammaw sang.

I knew the words to *In the Garden* before I even remember going to church. The first time it was played in our church, I was so pleased because I could sing along. I couldn't read yet so I couldn't follow the words in the hymn book, but when they played *In the Garden*, I sang as loud as anyone did.

Mammaw was the only grandparent still alive when I was born. She lived until my sixteenth birthday. When she died, one of the hymns that they played at her funeral was *In the Garden*. Every time I hear that song, I think of Mammaw.

As I sat there in the nursery listening to this hymn and looking at my son, I sang along silently. I thought back to the second verse when the singer said, "*I come to the garden alone.*" I have felt so alone through all of this. I retreated into prayer. The three of us being together as a family at this moment makes me think of the many ways we have been blessed and that God has protected us through these last two months.

While I was sitting there, one of the new dads carried his baby up to the window where his family was waiting. An elderly woman, I assume she must be a grandmother, held up a little girl who must be his daughter to see her new baby brother for probably the first time. There was no one at the window but the four of them. The mother stayed beside the crib. Looking at the three of them — grandmother, father, and daughter — standing there joined together as a family by the little baby — I can't help but appreciate how strong family ties are. This grandmother and little sister love the little baby who they have not yet held. They love the little baby as much as they love each other. That is the way I feel about Benjamin. I love him like I love my wife, my parents, and my sister. He makes us a family.

I suppose that is what a family really is — when you love someone you don't even know just because you are related.

APRIL 15

TODAY WAS A REAL BABY DAY. That is what I have started calling days when I forget that Benjamin is still sick and that we are still at the hospital. These are the days when I forget about all we have been through and what is yet to come. These are the days when it feels OK to let go of the apprehension that news the doctor tells us will be bad. These are the days when I remember that it is OK to breathe.

Nicki said that today was her best day ever. Work kept me from going to the hospital during the day, but Nicki gave me several telephone updates. The occupational therapist said that Benjamin was doing well, and the nurse practitioner, Kathy Fulton, said that Benjamin was tolerating his feedings and that if the doctor would agree, we could try an oral feeding.

Nicki grabbed Dr. Wooldridge and made a comment about how well Benjamin was tolerating the feedings and that he was pooping regularly. She gathered the courage to ask when we could try an oral feeding. Dr. Wooldridge surprised her by saying, "How about now?"

Nicki squealed with excitement, but chose not to do the feeding at 5:30 because she wanted to wait until I was there. With nervous anticipation, we waited for the 8:30 visit. When we arrived, the bottle was waiting for us.

Nicki held Benjamin when he took formula for the first time from a bottle. Actually I think he only took about half of the formula because half of it spilled onto his gown.

There is much more to the feeding process than a new father might suspect. First you have to find the baby's tongue and make sure that the nipple goes down on top of it rather than to the side or underneath. Then you have to squeeze his cheeks in order to get him to start sucking. Apparently this is not something premature babies do naturally. As if that is not enough, you then tilt the baby's head back and open the mouth by placing your thumb on the bottom of the chin and working it up an down in order to get the baby to swallow. Both mama and baby did wonderfully.

Benjamin reached up with both of his tiny hands and he grabbed her little finger and her thumb during the feeding. His most enjoyable time came when Nicki burped him for the first time. He loved it.

Nicki placed him on her shoulder with his head looking over toward me and she gently patted him on his back while she jiggled him up and down trying to get a burp. Benjamin held out as long as possible, enjoying his first "mommy ride." His eyes were half open and there was a trace of formula that bubbled out from his lips when he made a loud burping sound. All of this was, of course, captured on film.

THE LONG WAY HOME

It makes you wonder what we did before we had film and video to capture famous firsts. Everybody remembers their first kiss, their first car, and their first job, so I suppose that is why baby "firsts" are so important. Every book we buy talks about having a place to record baby's first haircut, first tooth, first time rolling over. It seems to me that too many of these activities are manufactured. Why should we really care about baby's first trip to the mall or baby's first fast food?

I look back at the book that Mom and Pop kept for me that recorded my firsts. There were about eight of them. At the risk of sounding hypocritical, I have already filled up half of Benjamin's book concerning the popular movies, important news events, and the music of the times. Looking back at my own, I suddenly feel much older than I really am. Marilyn Monroe was the popular movie star and the dance was "The Twist." The big news event was Kennedy's assassination. We had not even made it into space yet.

I look back at the news events that I remember growing up and you really do remember where you are at certain moments. I remember watching the first moon walk, Watergate, Nixon's resignation, and the explosion of the space shuttle and what I was doing when Elvis died. What's even worse is that Nicki was not even born when most of these events occurred.

I am now able to add April 15, 1999 to the list because at 8:52 that evening, I was sitting in a rocking chair on the fifth floor of Children's Hospital in the NICU with a camcorder in my right hand, recording my wife burping our first child.

To add to the festivities, Nicki and I did the first unassisted mama to daddy transfer. It would have been perfect except I knocked his hat off onto the floor. Today has been a good baby day.

APRIL 16

I AM IN THE "ZONE." This is the feeling basketball players have when no one can guard them. Home-run hitters describe the ball as looking like a watermelon when it comes across the plate. In the NICU, it means everything is clicking.

Perfect days are measured by the details. A truly great day is not made up of magnificent events, but it is a combination of the little things that come together to make a truly perfect day.

Our day began when Nicki arrived at the hospital and found out that Esther would be the nurse. When Nicki arrived for the morning update, there was absolutely no bad news. Esther said that everything looked great, Benjamin was tolerating his feedings well, and he was ready for mama to give him his 11:30 bottle.

Nicki stayed with Benjamin from 9:30 until 6:00. She and Esther played with Benjamin and talked about life. The two of them picked out Benjamin's morning outfit and laid out an outfit for him to be changed into at nighttime. All of the nurses made a pilgrimage to his crib to talk about how great he was looking. Several of them wanted to hold him. When I arrived around 5:30, it was easy to tell that everyone's spirits were high.

The mood was relaxed, almost jocular. Nicki and Esther both cut up with me, and they talked about what a handsome young man Benjamin had become now that they were able to clean up all of the flaked skin that had accumulated during the long stretch while he was on the ventilator.

During the dinner break, Ashley and Claudette threw us a baby shower at Claudette's parents' church. This is the only baby shower that I have gotten to go to and I had a blast. Many of my long-time friends were there, and for many of them it was the first time that I had the opportunity to talk to them since Benjamin had been in the hospital. They did a great job of asking few questions and just letting us know how much they loved us and were thinking of us. Being with these friends and opening presents was like being part of a huge family.

My friend, Dr. Sexton, had been by the hospital to see Benjamin and left a note indicating he had been there. He and I have had many talks about fatherhood and medicine. There were many times in my life that I went to him and his wife for advice and the advice was always good. His wife, Carol, is also a nurse. When I had a crush on their daughter, I would go by their house in the mornings and have breakfast. Carol would listen to my plans and make me feel like part of their family.

That night when we got back to the hospital, Benjamin kept his eyes open for almost the entire visit. Nicki put him to sleep by rocking him in the rocking chair. I got to hold him for a long time, and he would grab both of my hands with his fingers.

Nicki gave him a bath that made him clean and beautiful. His little baby outfits make him look like an ad for the *Baby Superstore*. This feels right — easy — like it's supposed to be.

APRIL 17

WHEN WE AWOKE THIS MORNING, we found that our water main had burst and there was no way to shower. We had to go to Ashley and Claudette's house to get ready and did not arrive at the hospital until a little before 2:00.

We only had time for a quick walk-through visit because a new baby had arrived, but when we came back, the news was huge. The doctors were going to discontinue Benjamin's intravenous liquid nutrition feedings and go to all oral feedings. Also, he had had three bowel movements.

It was wonderful the way the nurses treated us. The nurse practitioner came over during our visit and told us that another new baby was on the way. She then commented that since Stage I was already full, one of the babies would have to be moved over to Stage II, and she felt that it was going to be Benjamin. We got so excited that when Dr. Wooldridge said Benjamin needed to be moved to Stage II because he was doing so well, I almost kissed him. Dr. Wooldridge thinks it is time for Benjamin to move to Stage II because they need his bed for more critical babies. Nicki and I cried.

Not only did we get to move to Stage II, but we are also in the far back corner with Benjamin's buddy Coulter. The only other baby in that corner was Patrick.

In actuality, the total distance of Benjamin's move was only a few feet. Since he was already near the end of the section, they moved him across the intersecting hall to the first bed in the back part of Stage II — a distance of only fifteen feet. The whole process only took a matter of minutes. Suddenly we were in a corner away from all of the commotion of Stage I.

Growing up, I always wanted to be an astronaut. Every Halloween, when it came time to pick the costume that was what I chose. Even to this day, I love everything about the astronauts. I read the books, watch the movies, and if I had my life to live over, I would be an astronaut.

I remember when Neil Armstrong landed on the moon and what a big deal it was. My entire family gathered together and sat around the television and watched. Participating in the move from Stage I to Stage II reminded me of his famous statement, This is one small step for man, one giant leap for mankind. This move was one small step for Benjamin, but one giant leap for the morale of his parents!

Although nothing had really changed by moving from Stage I to Stage II, our morale soared. This was a step toward going home. It was a vote of confidence from the nurses and doctors that Benjamin was doing well enough that he did not have to be under constant care.

One of the big differences between Stage I and Stage II is the responsibility of the nurses. At Stage I, a nurse is always present. When you visit, they will try to sit off to the side, but they do not stray from their patient. In Stage II, the nurses are dealing with multiple babies and do not have to constantly monitor their patients.

Also, in Stage II you can pick up your baby any time. You don't have to ask permission. You don't have to ask for help. You just reach in and grab him. In Stage I, you would be beaten if you reached in and picked up your baby.

As I was basking in the euphoria of the moment, after we had settled into our new home and Nicki had proudly snatched Benjamin up, changed his outfit, and started rocking him, I proceeded to do my daily review of his chart. While I was reading the nurses' notes, I saw a notation from Andrea, our nurse the previous evening, stating that I did not understand the purpose of one of the medicines. This amazed me.

Andrea was referring to an off-hand comment I made about one of the medicines that was incorrect. I assumed the medicine did a particular thing, when in fact it was for something else. This was a minor comment that I thought had probably gone unnoticed. Showing how perceptive these NICU nurses are, she made a note in the record so that the doctor would explain to me during the next visit what that medicine did. What makes these nurses so effective is that they perceive everything. This is why the survival rate of the babies is so high — these nurses are trained to notice even the minor changes.

That is my number one criticism of doctors today. They do not spend time with their patients and they make an off-hand diagnosis and prescribe medicines without really taking the time to know what is going on with their patient. The medical malpractice cases that I handle are always a result of a doctor who did not spend enough time with the patient to do his or her job. Time is what separates the good doctors from the bad.

The doctors and nurses that we encountered at Children's Hospital are some of the best health care providers that I have ever seen. They spend a great deal of time observing and making notes of any changes, so that they can make an accurate diagnosis. Likewise, they are incredibly thorough. No stone goes unturned when it comes to trying to figure out what is wrong. The commitment of these health care providers is extraordinary.

My experience with Children's Hospital has been limited to Benjamin, but I cannot imagine ever taking him anywhere else. These health care providers could serve as a standard by which all other doctors and nurses could be measured.

We had a long visit with Benjamin and couldn't wait to come back in the evening. It is so much quieter on this side. Everybody's mood is upbeat. Nicki and I have practically been dancing all day.

While Robert and Coby were gone for dinner, I watched Robert's dad experience an A&B spell with Coulter. When Coulter quit breathing, and the monitor went off, Grandpa got the big eye. Much of his response mimicked mine from a few days ago when I gently tried to wake Benjamin. He gently spoke to Coulter, trying to rouse him. When he became aware that all of us were watching him, including the nurses, his face immediately flushed. Again, he gently shook Coulter and whispered, "Come on Coulter, come on." After a few seconds, one of the nurses interceded and gave Coulter a hard shake to get him breathing again. I couldn't help but grin.

I was pleased to know that someone else shared my inability to be anything but gentle with these babies. One of things that I am going to have to realize is that babies won't break. Coulter's grandpa is one of the first people I remember from this whole ordeal. He was the first family member of another baby that I spoke with. Before Benjamin was delivered, and Nicki was being treated on the Sixth Floor at Fort Sanders Hospital, I met Mr. Eldridge prior to Coulter being born. He is a likable man and from looking in his eyes, I could tell he was a good man. Like my father, he is going to be a great grandparent.

These past four days have been a whirlwind of activity. Benjamin has gone from being on the ventilator, to being off the ventilator and receiving the feedings through a tube, to being in Stage II and having only bottle feedings. It is truly miraculous.

I capped off the evening by participating in my first non-nurse pick up from the crib. I did it totally unassisted. I am beginning to think that maybe I have the "right stuff" to be a dad.

APRIL 18

BENJAMIN LOVES BEING HELD. Maybe it is because we have not been able to hold him as much as we would have liked, but he does not like it when Nicki or I put him down. He becomes fussy and wants to be picked up. This plays right into Nicki's hands because she looks for any excuse to hold him.

I didn't arrive at the hospital until after Mock Trial practice, but Nicki had gone to the hospital as soon as she woke up. When I got there, she was rocking Benjamin and Robert was rocking Coulter while Coby looked on. I watched the three of them for several minutes before I went in and sat down. Coby was resting her eyes and Robert and Nicki had the babies tucked across their shoulders, gently patting them, looking past everything else, lost in the quietness of the moment. Everything seemed to fit. After I arrived, the four of us just sat there and shared time with our sons.

One of the nurses has actually used the "home" word! The only thing still in Benjamin is the subclavian port — a permanent intravenous port for medicine. As soon as that is removed, he will be wire- and tube-free.

The subclavian port is the only thing keeping him from having a regular bath. Nicki gave him another sponge bath today and changed his outfit. We have to be careful when we put his clothes on so we don't pull the subclavian out.

The reason that Benjamin had a subclavian inserted in the first place was that he has had so many needle sticks in his hands, arms, feet, and head that the nurses had lost the ability to get a good i.v. line. The subclavian is surgically attached, so that the medicine can be put directly in without having to stick him with a needle each time. The doctors have indicated this will come out any day now.

Now that the nurses are using the "home" word, they tell us that we better start scheduling our classes. Before a baby can go home, the parents and grandparents have to take infant CPR and monitor classes. Benjamin will come home on a heart and breathing monitor. This will involve a small cuff that will be placed around his foot. It will act just like the monitors here in the hospital so that if he has an A&B spell during the night, the monitor will go off and we can give any assistance that is necessary.

We do not know how long Benjamin will have to be on the monitor. Some babies are on it for almost a year — some go off within a matter of weeks. Benjamin will be assigned a home health care worker who will come out each month and download the information from the monitor to a central computer system. This data will measure how many A&B spells he has had and his heart and breathing rates so that they can decide when the monitor can be removed.

The infant CPR classes are a good idea, although nothing that the doctors and nurses have told us would give us any reason to suspect that we would ever need to perform CPR. But it's still a good skill to have. Benjamin's size and weight are enough to allow him to go home, if the doctors can get everything else under control.

We finished the evening in much the same way that we began it — holding Benjamin. Nicki rocked him while I sat quietly watching. His head is nestled in that soft spot against her neck and his right arm is draped over her arm. His eyes are closed and she is quiet, trying not to disturb him as she rocks slowly back and forth.

As much as she likes holding him, and he likes being held, I think I enjoy watching the two of them even more. It is so comforting for me to be a part of this moment — a moment that I did not think would ever come.

APRIL 19

EVERYONE GOT CHOCOLATE-COVERED strawberries today. In East Tennessee, in the spring, one of the local candy manufacturers makes chocolate-covered strawberries. They are similar to chocolate-covered cherries, except much more elegant.

They take whole fresh strawberries and dip them in chocolate. Cream sauce is injected inside the strawberries. The cream sauce, similar to the sugar filling in a chocolate-covered cherry, makes these strawberries a "taste explosion." As a treat to all of the nurses, Benjamin, through his mother, bought chocolate-covered strawberries for everybody.

The best way to eat these strawberries, if your mouth is big enough, is to put the whole thing in your mouth and bite down. The juice will go everywhere if you try to take just a bite of it. The chocolate-covered berry is about the size of a golf ball, so you have to make a chipmunk mouth to get it all in. They are incredible.

The nurses and doctors have done so much for us that we need to try to do something for them. Everybody is always bringing cookies and snacks, but these berries are such a well-kept secret (all of us that eat them try to keep them for ourselves) that we felt we would introduce the staff to the best taste sensation in East Tennessee. The strawberries were a huge success.

By the time we arrived at the hospital, Benjamin's permanent subclavian port had been removed. This meant that Benjamin does not have any permanent lines going into him.

I did get a bit of a scare today when Esther told me that Benjamin had a heart murmur. This is something that Nicki had not shared with me. When Esther saw my reaction, she must have spoken to one of the doctors because Dr. Prinz came shortly to talk with me.

Dr. Prinz indicated that he was not concerned about the heart murmur because Benjamin had already had so many echocardiograms because of the SVTs that he felt Benjamin's heart was structurally sound. He indicated that the murmur was something Benjamin would probably grow out of. But if not, it could be something that he would have for the rest of his life, without it causing any problems. He said that the word murmur has a tendency to scare people, but it is not unusual for many adults that have no heart problems to have a heart murmur.

This was another instance when the nurses were aware that I needed a little reassurance and they passed a cue to the doctor so that he could come in and explain everything.

Dr. Prinz is pretty much the grandfather of the unit. He is the senior partner in the practice and he seems to take a lot of pride in his patient interaction. He is an excellent physician and a great people person. He is not afraid to hug. I can tell that he genuinely cares about me.

During my visit, I watched the parents of baby Jasmine, a baby who has been moved in across from us, visit her for the first time. Jasmine has done so well that she did not spend but a few minutes in Stage I and has been moved to Stage II to be a feeder/grower. When her parents came in today, they were concerned because the doctors were using phototherapy (a heat lamp) because Jasmine has a mild jaundice condition. It scared them to death.

I wanted to tell them that jaundice is nothing! It surprises me how quickly, although this is our fifty-fourth day in the hospital, not counting the time Nicki's spent before Benjamin was born, that I have become numb — deadened, I guess — to all of the tragedy surrounding us.

I fought the urge to go over and tell them that this was not anything to worry about, because no matter what I said, they were still going to worry. That is just part of being a parent. And part of being a good neighbor in the NICU is not telling other parents that their problems are not life threatening or not a concern.

All of our babies have problems or we would not be here. It is so infuriating to have someone tell me not to worry. I can't help but worry. I would not be normal if I didn't worry.

Baby Jasmine was going to be fine, but part of the parenting process is that these people needed to be allowed to worry about their daughter just as we have worried about Benjamin.

Many of the mothers of the babies in the NICU are young girls, who can't be more than eighteen or nineteen years old, with no husband or family support. Nicki and I have truly been blessed to have my parents and her mom and dad to help us through all of this. Also, we have had our extended family and friends, including the people that I work with, who have made this situation bearable.

It saddens me to watch the tragedy and sorrow of the other moms and dads, but it is exhilarating to watch the victories. Where I sit in the corner of the nursery, I can watch everything that happens. Whenever good news is given, I can see the hand pumps of the fathers and the tears of joy and relief streaming down the faces of the mothers.

Hearing a parent laugh or seeing them smile makes everything great. Although these moments are offset by tragedy and bad news — in some cases horrific news — laughs help put everything into a sort of perspective.

Tonight my visit was cut down to almost nothing because right after we got there, Darrell and Judy arrived. Darrell held Benjamin for the first time. This is somewhat ironic for me. Darrell holds Benjamin so easily. Darrell picked him up just like he is supposed to. My Pop has been afraid to hold Benjamin because of the tubes and wire. During the day visit, Esther told Pop that tomorrow he would have to hold Benjamin — no matter what.

I don't push Pop because everything comes in its own time and with its own purpose. Tonight, everything is great because the reality of Benjamin coming home is finally becoming a real possibility. It could be within a month. So I sat in the waiting room, confident that Darrell, Judy, and Nicki were holding Benjamin and the nurses were eating strawberries.

APRIL 20

COBY'S MOTHER, who is visiting from Florida, left their freezer door open and ruined over 200 bottles of breast milk that Coby has been stockpiling since Coulter's birth. Coby is not happy.

Coulter has been through as much, if not more, as Benjamin has during the past two months. Coulter was put on a ventilator immediately after birth. Coby told me it was torture for her to not be able to be with him during those first few hours. She was recovering from the delivery, so Robert acted as a courier, going back and forth between Children's Hospital and Fort Sanders Hospital with news about Coulter's progress.

THE LONG WAY HOME

When Coby came to the NICU the day after Coulter was born, her first thought was that he was smaller than she thought he would be. She had many of the same feelings that Nicki and I had — not knowing whether to feel excited, sad, or angry. After the first ultrasound, she and Robert were told that Coulter had an IVH (intraventricular hemorrhage). It is a Grade I.

Even though Coulter is so sick — the nurses call him a "don't touch" baby — Coby was brought into the "mother" process early. She was able to change a diaper on day two. She and Robert had been able to hold Coulter for the first time on February 25, the day Benjamin was born.

Coulter did really well during his first week. It was not until he was a week old that Robert and Coby learned that the IVH was worse. Another ultrasound revealed that he now had a Grade III hemorrhage on each side of his brain. Dr. Buchheit explained to them what that meant. He gave them a best-case/worst-case scenario. If Coulter could correct the problem on his own, the doctors would not have to do anything. If the hemorrhages continued and developed into Grade IV, then Coulter could have brain damage.

Coby told me that she felt like she had been kicked in the stomach. In the NICU, bad news seems to come in waves. While the doctors monitored the hemorrhages, they were also treating Coulter for jaundice. Ultimately, Coulter did have a shunt put in his brain to control the bleeding and had another surgery for reflux. Thankfully, he survived both procedures and was soon moved to the "real baby" zone.

Tonight seems ordinary. Nicki changed an exceptionally messy diaper this afternoon. In the process, Benjamin reached down and grabbed a handful of poop and proceeded to spread it across his head. The more that Nicki tried to clean it up, the worse it got. Ultimately the bathtub had to be brought out.

I left my wife to clean up what I suspect is the first of many such messes to attend the annual volleyball coaches' meeting to set up next year's schedule. I have coached high school volleyball for over 20 years. Jeff Harshbarger is the head coach, but he was in Washington with students from the middle school where he teaches. The other coaches were tied up with family commitments. So, since I was already in Knoxville, I agreed to attend the coaches' meeting.

Our team finished third in the state competition last year and is a pre-season number one pick for this year. Because the coaching staff is so competitive, we are not very popular with the other coaching staffs. My mission at the meeting was fairly simple — fill up the remainder of our schedule and see if the other district had any objection to our district hosting the regional tournament.

Our region is comprised of two districts. The powerhouse in the other district is Gibbs High School — one of our strongest foes. Each year the two districts take turns hosting the regional tournament. It was not our turn, but the Gibbs High School coach had already said he did not want to host the tournament. I did not think there would be any objection to our district sponsoring the event.

THE LONG WAY HOME

When the regional meeting began, I threw this idea out, having spoken with the coaches from all the other schools, except for Christian Academy of Knoxville. Christian Academy is a fairly new private school in our area that has only recently added a volleyball team. They are not competitive yet and were not even expected to participate in the regional tournament.

A high school volleyball tournament is a lot of work for the host team, but the revenue is split equally among the participants. Therefore, the only reason to host the tournament is if your team has a chance of winning. Christian Academy had not been expected to have a winning season, much less participate in a regional tournament. I was stunned when their coach torpedoed my suggestion.

In fact, she even ridiculed me during the meeting and demanded an immediate vote be taken for Christian Academy to host the tournament. When the vote was successful, she punched her fist in the air and said, "Yes!" I wanted to disappear. Maybe Christian Academy will somehow upset one of the teams in their district so that we can beat them in the regional tournament on their home floor. If we do, I will want to dance around her, pump my fist, and make that comment about being careful what you wish for! But that night at the coaches' meeting, all I could do was lower my head, accept my disappointment, and slink back to the hospital.

The evening visit went smoothly. We had dinner with Coulter's parents and talked about the day's misadventures. It is the first time, in a long time, we did not talk about our sons' health problems. It is refreshing to be able to focus on concerns other than whether or not your child will die. Spoiled milk, messy diapers, and public ridicule are nothing compared to having surgery or being put on life support.

My whole perspective about what is a problem and what is an inconvenience has changed. It is amazing what a serious illness can do to make you look forward to late night feedings, crying fits, and the other hassles that come with having a newborn. I make a promise today that I will never begrudge Benjamin, or Nicki, my full attention when it comes to these minor inconveniences. In fact, I think that I welcome these inconveniences.

Nicki read a story in one of those *Chicken Soup* books that hit home. It involved a six-year-old boy who saw a sign in the window of a pet store that said "Puppies for sale — 50¢." The boy, obviously poor, walked in and put his two quarters on the counter and said that he wanted to pick out a puppy. The shopkeeper took him to the box where six puppies were being kept. The boy carefully made his selection and picked a small one in the back.

When the man saw his selection, he told the boy to pick another one because this puppy was lame. Sure enough, the puppy had been born with a deformed foot that caused him to drag his left leg. The boy refused, saying this was the puppy that he wanted. The man then told the boy to keep the fifty cents — he could just have the puppy. At this point, tears welled up in the boy's eyes and he pulled the puppy to his chest. He pointed down to his own foot, held straight by two rigid metal braces, and said that just because the puppy was lame, it did not mean that it was worth less than the other puppies.

As I rock my son to sleep and think about what lies ahead, I don't know how the cerebral palsy will affect him or what other health complications he might have as a result of his sickness. All I know is that he is worth as much as any other baby in the world — to me he is worth even more. I love him.

APRIL 21

TODAY WAS BENJAMIN'S DUE DATE. If he had not developed problems, the doctors predicted that he would be born on April 21. When Nicki called from the hospital to check in with me, it was obvious she had been crying. She feels guilty for not being able to carry Benjamin to full term.

Her best friend Jenny sent her flowers and the nurses tried to console her, but it is hard. When she sees Leslie still pregnant and Claudette with Riley, who was delivered routinely, it makes her sad. Although the doctors have told her that nothing she did caused Benjamin's problems, there is something about delivering Benjamin early that makes her feel as if she did not fulfill her role as a mother.

Nicki has done so much during the past two months. She has fought through the trauma of possibly losing Benjamin, not once, but twice. She has had to modify her entire life. Instead of bringing him home on time and making bottles, changing diapers, and doing the things that she learned about in parenting classes, she gets up every morning and goes to the NICU to sit beside his bedside.

Benjamin has never known a home other than the hospital. Nicki and I have never been alone with him. He has never been in the dark. He has never been in a place where there is absolute quiet. The only life that Benjamin has known has been hospital life. He has been fed for the most part through tubes, and for most of his life, he has been kept alive by machines.

He has already had more injections than I will ever have. He has had more blood transfusions and received more medicine than I have received in my lifetime.

Nicki and I don't know anyone who has had a child in the intensive care. All of our friends who have had babies brought their babies home. All of our family has healthy children — children that are, for lack of a better word, normal. That life is foreign to the both of us.

April 21 is nothing more than just another day on a calendar, but at our house, every calendar had that day circled with the words "Ben's due date" written inside the square. All of our plans had been made around this date. I had blocked this time off of my calendar so that I could be at the hospital for the wondrous event.

Nicki scheduled this semester in law school so she could be a regular mom for a few weeks before going back to school. Everything about the pregnancy was textbook — perfect. There were no signs that Benjamin was sick — nothing to indicate that he could be premature. It just happened.

Yesterday, the worst school shooting in our nation's history occurred in Colorado. I stayed up watching *Nightline* as they interviewed the survivors and talked about the shooters. I am sure that when the students went to school yesterday morning, they thought that it would be a day just like every other day. They would take tests, make plans for the weekend, and some of them would talk about college. I am sure that none of them thought that their plans would include the funerals of their friends. I am sure that the families who were preparing to lose a child to graduation did not know that they would be losing a child forever. I am sure that no one really suspected that the killers were just that — killers — not just unhappy students who did not fit in.

When I look at a tragedy that is so unexpected, I don't know which hits harder — the loss or the fact that there is no explanation of why. With Benjamin, there is not one thing we could have done to prepare us for what we have been through and nothing that has happened has given us any explanation of why.

This afternoon my Pop finally held Benjamin for the first time. Pop was with Nicki and Benjamin when I called her at the nursery. She had Benjamin in her arms and used this time for an excuse to hand him to Pop. All of this has been so hard on my father. I have only seen him cry two or three times in my entire life. When he talks about the struggle that Benjamin has been through, tears fill his eyes and his voice breaks. He looks for words that aren't there — that don't need to be there.

My Pop is unable to say why he is hurting and he doesn't know what to do to stop his pain — he just knows that he suffers because Benjamin suffers. Watching him deal with this is like looking in a mirror. I see myself when I look at him. Just like my Pop, I am unsure how to hold Benjamin, how gentle to be, how to talk to my wife about what has happened or what will happen. I don't know how to deal with the fact that things are not going to be like what we thought they would be when we circled in April 21 on the calendar. Everything that has happened since we first learned that Benjamin was sick changes everything we expected. When I look at the calendar, starting with tomorrow, everything is unknown. No more blocks have been filled in — none should be filled in. If anything, Benjamin has made me realize that nothing is certain — even if there will be a tomorrow. The calendar should be no more than a way to measure time — it should not be a place to record expectations.

I keep a calendar at my office that is filled with trial dates, appointments, and reminders of important events. For the most part, all of these things are written in pencil because things change. Appointments are cancelled. Trial dates are moved. When this information is erased from the calendar, it is as if it never happened. I wish that I had written Benjamin's due date in pencil, but there it is on the calendar on the wall in the nursery in big red letters — a reminder of what was expected and of what went wrong. Since it is written in pen, it can never be removed — merely marked over or whited out. It will always be there no matter what we try to do to hide it or forget it.

It doesn't really matter though because the calendar is nothing but a reminder — and reminders are just that — reminders. They have no significance, no real importance. Nothing we could have done would have made Benjamin come any later. Benjamin is still alive, we are still his parents, and one day the room where that calendar hangs will be his room. On May 1, the page will be turned and a new month will begin. One day, around the first of the year, the calendar will be taken down and discarded. Depending on how many keepsakes we save, a decision will be made about whether to throw away the calendar or just store it along with clothes that no longer fit, toys that are outdated, and cards of congratulation or condolence. Either way, the calendar will become a memory.

I don't think that it is bad to remember. In a few years, if it's that long, I will forget what Benjamin's due date was. My memory will fade as to what happened in the hospital. And when we tell the story, all we will say is that Benjamin was sick before he got to come home. Today, though, Nicki and I will take just a moment to remember what was expected and to be thankful for what we have.

APRIL 22

HOME. We are starting to hear this word a lot. All of the nurses are telling us that Benjamin is progressing so quickly that we need to start thinking about taking him home.

I probably have never prayed so hard in my life as I have prayed these past two months. My prayers have been simple — that Benjamin would live. Now that I believe he is going to live, I am faced with the realization that the place he is going to be living — soon — will be with me.

My experience with babies has been absolutely zero. Benjamin is the first baby I have fed and I still have not changed his diaper. To hear the nurses and staff talk about taking him home, particularly after all that we have been through, is overwhelming.

Nicki has taken to being a mother quite naturally. All of this stuff they say about maternal instincts is true. That also explains why nothing is ever said about paternal instincts —

because there aren't any. I have absolutely no instincts about how to act — nothing comes naturally.

I have become an information sponge. I read everything. I go across the street to the regular nursery where there is a place called Teddy Bear University, a four-hour course for expectant fathers. I take everything I can find — every flier, every piece of paper, every scribbled note that has been discarded.

On my way back to the NICU after foraging for information, I saw Rod in the hallway. Rod and I are old friends from law school ten years ago. I have seen him only once since then, but when our eyes met, there was instant recognition.

The last time I saw Rod was about two years after I graduated. I was going to northern Ohio to do some church work and stopped at a McDonalds outside of Pittsburgh. When I sat down to eat my burger, I saw Rob and his mother. For some reason, it didn't seem unusual that our paths had crossed. It didn't dawn on us immediately just how unusual it was that we would meet at the same McDonalds so far from home. I had the same type of feeling then that I had when I saw Rod in the hallway.

Rod and his wife have a premature baby named John who has just been delivered and is on his way to the NICU. I immediately told him we were already there and started anticipating his questions. Our catch-up time was great. I told him that once he and his wife got settled in at the NICU, I would be sure to check on them.

I made it back to the nursery for the 8:30 feeding. Benjamin went through his bottle in about 15 minutes — a new record. The night nurse bragged on him and talked about how much Esther loved Benjamin and how Esther would rearrange the morning schedule so that she could be with him each day.

This made Nicki feel incredibly special because of the relationship that she and Esther have established. I just wish that I could convince Esther to quit her job at the NICU and come live with the Cantrell's until Benjamin is up and about. But that isn't going to happen, so I have decided that it's time I found a book on how to change a diaper.

A P R I L   2 3

I DID A BAD THING TODAY — the kind of bad thing that stays with you — the kind of thing you regret doing as soon as you do it, but you are stuck with it. The feeling is like when you throw a baseball and realize it is going to break a window, but you can't grab it back. Or when you slam the car door shut just as you realize that your car keys are locked inside.

I had dropped Nicki off at the hospital after dinner to run a couple of errands. I was late getting back and got caught up in the evening rush of visitors trying to get into the scrub-in room. A couple ahead of me in line was taking forever to scrub-in. I already had a gown on and was waiting my turn in line. A woman behind me politely tapped me on the shoulder and told me that I needed to scrub-in before I went inside. I quickly told her that I had been here for over nine weeks and that I knew the procedure. I was short to the point of being rude.

I hurriedly scrubbed-in and made my way to Benjamin's crib. As I was settling in for my visit, I looked in horror as the woman made her way back to the bed of a baby just across the way from us in Stage I where Benjamin had been. She was the baby's mother. From watching how the nurses dealt with this woman — the mother — I knew the baby was sick. I was immediately overcome with shame. To complicate matters even more, the grandmother of this little girl is one of the nicest persons I have ever met. The grandmother came over and commented on how pretty Benjamin looked and apologized for her daughter telling me about scrubbing.

I fumbled for words of apology, but came up short. When I saw the mother go out to the waiting room so her husband could come in and visit, I purposefully made an excuse to go to the lounge. I caught up with her in the hallway and again mumbled an apology. I then asked how her baby daughter was and found out that she had sepsis just like Benjamin. I told her about Benjamin's experience and it seemed to brighten her spirits a little bit. She apologized to me again and I told her there was no need — then she asked me to pray for her little girl. I felt even worse.

When I went back to the scrub-in room, I heard someone calling my name. I looked up and saw Wes, another law school classmate. I assumed like Rod, he must have a baby in the NICU, but he was there to visit his good friends the Eldridges. As I began to explain our relationship with the Eldridges, a man came up to us. Wes introduced him to me. He is the brother of another law school classmate and also a friend of the Eldridges. I am stunned at how small this world is that we live in and how everything seems to intersect.

The nurses are beginning to talk about Benjamin coming home within a couple of weeks. There is no way that I am ready. As I say my evening prayers, which include the little girl and her mother, I pray for patience and strength to be ready. As a way of atonement, I also wrote a long letter to Rod and his wife trying to detail some of the experiences and fears I have had during the past two months. I slipped it into his son's chart while they were gone so that they could read it first thing in the morning. Maybe that's how we get through this — by sharing things with each other.

APRIL 24

I CHANGED MY FIRST DIAPER TONIGHT. With the typical luck of the Irish, it was a pee-only diaper, but I sweated like I was performing major surgery. Because of the length of Benjamin's stay, we have achieved somewhat of a celebrity status in the nursery. Coby made sure that everyone around witnessed my performance. One of the respiratory therapists came over and put his hand on my shoulder and told me that I did a great job. I was just glad to get it over with.

Nicki and the nurses had been putting a tremendous amount of pressure on me to do my first diaper change. I had studied how they did it, how they lifted Benjamin, and cleaned his bottom with a wipe, and how they tucked the edges of the diaper under so it wouldn't leak. Now that I have experienced a diaper change first hand, I can tell you that it is a lot like fishing — it doesn't matter how many books you read or what anybody tells you, there is no substitute for actually taking the rod in hand and casting a line. I made up my mind weeks ago that the first diaper change I did was going to be a solo because I do not respond well to someone looking over my shoulder. To say that Nicki would be giving me a lot of instruction is an understatement. For me, the best way to do it was to just jump in feet first and give it a go.

So, it was with a great deal of pride that I showed off my handiwork to Nicki when she arrived about 30 minutes later from a baby shower. She could see that my chest was swelled with pride as I proudly told her what I had done unassisted. She said that she knew that because I had put the diaper on backward and that for future reference, the funny designs go on the front.

After Nicki arrived, we settled into our evening routine of chatting with Coulter's parents. I spent some time looking around the nursery. I was pleased to learn that the baby whose mother I had been so short with yesterday did not have sepsis after all, but merely an intestinal problem. She was doing much better. I watched her hold her child for the first time. Of course, the nurse was Nancy, whose strength is letting you know that everything is OK. She pulled the old "I need you to hold your child while I change her bed routine." I have learned this is one of her standbys. Nancy caught me looking at her while this was going on and gave me a wink to let me know I was in on her secret.

Across the way from Benjamin — still in a room by himself — Brandon has apparently taken a turn for the worse. He is so swollen that they keep him covered. I watched as his parents cried openly at his bedside for over an hour. This has been such a long ordeal for the two of them.

Sometime during the visit, there was about a fifteen-minute interlude when Nicki was feeding Benjamin, Coulter's parents were snuggling with him, and Brandon's parents were crying that I took just a moment to look around the nursery. All of the parents were focused on their child. The nurses were either working with their patients or busying themselves with any one of a thousand things they have to do each evening.

There was a peace over the entire nursery. Not peace as in silence, because it is never quiet in the NICU, but the peace that comes with acceptance. Even though some parents were up and others were down, we all shared a time of peace. There are not many of these moments in the NICU. I have been here long enough to know how to appreciate one when it happens. There is so much emotion in the families that love these 36 little patients and it is rare for us to have a time of peace.

I suppose that as a father it won't be much different for me as Benjamin grows up. There will be good times and bad times, times of celebration and times of mourning, and times of frustration. Times that he and I see eye to eye and times that we push each other away. But amidst all of these times, there will also be times of peace. It will be these times of peace when we are so close we don't have to talk — like the comfortable silence that comes after you are married and you drive somewhere, not talking, but not worried about why your spouse isn't saying anything. These moments are comfortable and they get us through the storms.

APRIL 25

NICKI WENT TO THE HOSPITAL while I went to Mock Trial practice. Dr. Buchheit told Nicki that if Benjamin kept improving, he might be able to go home as early as Thursday or Friday. She called me about 2:00 p.m. with the news. I was so excited that I called Harshbarger to take me to the hospital so that I could be with Nicki and Benjamin.

When I arrived, Nicki was teary when she told me the news. She said that Dr. Buchheit thought Benjamin was doing great and he saw no reason why we should not be able to leave by the end of the week. Dr. Buchheit had removed the nasogastric feeding tube. For the first time since Benjamin had been sick, he had no tubes in him. We were able to take him over to the observation window.

For so long I have watched the other dads take their babies to the observation window that faced out into the hallway to show them off to friends and family members who were not allowed to come inside. For some reason, it was always the dads that performed this function. I don't ever recall seeing a mother take a baby to the window. Most of the things in the nursery are geared to the mothers, but this honor is reserved for the dads.

I practically bounced through the nursery as I took Benjamin down the aisle between the Stage I beds — past where he had been for two months — during that time when I didn't know if he would live or die. I took him past the other parents who were still awaiting some sign that it would be OK to start living and quit preparing for a tragedy that may never come. While I walked toward the window, I wanted to stop at every bed and show Benjamin to the other moms and dads — to let them know that everything would be OK — that their baby would get better just like Benjamin got better — that it was OK to hope — that it was OK to think about their first day of school, their first car, even grandchildren. I wanted to put Benjamin in the crib beside their babies so that they could see what was ahead — so that they could escape from the present.

As I walked toward the window, I wanted to take Benjamin around to all of the nurses, doctors, and respiratory therapists who had played such a huge part in saving his life. I didn't know how to thank these people. I don't know how to do anything else but show him off. Every nurse I passed would smile. If they had been one of the nurses who had cared for Benjamin, they commented on how well he looked and that he looked like me.

For the first time in weeks, I was not afraid to look deep into their eyes because I knew what I would be seeing was life. The reservation that had been present before — when they were so careful not to get my hopes up or Nicki's hopes up — when they tried to be gentle telling us about sepsis and cerebral palsy — was now gone. It has been replaced by a brightness that comes when they realize it's safe to have fun. It's OK for us to start planning again. It's OK for us to think about home and not have to think about taking down his crib and repainting the walls.

Since Benjamin had been sick, the door to the nursery has been closed. Nicki and I avoid it even though our house is small. It has not been that long ago that our families gathered together to clean and paint. Nicki and the grandmothers had carefully selected all sorts of Winnie the Pooh decorations in little boy patterns. Nicki and I went to *Home Depot* to select the right shade of blinds that complimented the bright pattern of the wallpaper.

Nicki, Jenny, Claudette, and Leslie had discussed the pros and cons of different types of decorations and ornaments. I remember how happy Nicki was when she found three balloons at the *Baby Superstore* that matched the balloons that were in all the decorations.

I remember how long I searched for a net to suspend in the corner to hold all of Benjamin's stuffed animals — animals that were bought in anticipation of his arrival — animals he had never seen.

Nicki was so excited when we found a small ceiling fan with colored arms and a bright light in the middle. She was so anxious to make sure the room was ready for his arrival.

Pop came over one night and assembled the crib. We had selected a light maple color that would transform into a bed when Benjamin got old enough to stand up. Nicki had chosen light colors because she felt the room should be a little boy's room, bright and fun.

I had never seen a changing table. I didn't know there were such things until we found one that matched his bed and chest of drawers. I also learned about Diaper Genies™. We even bought a dehumidifier so that the air in the room would not be too damp. It took us weeks to get his room ready. I painted the ceiling myself and even painted the bathroom, too.

But once Benjamin got sick, all of the joy that had gone into creating that room was replaced with dread. I knew how difficult it would be to take everything down — to repaint all of the walls — to store the furniture. I knew all of these things would have to be done or Nicki and I would go insane because the room would be a constant reminder.

Today, though, all of that has been forgotten because I was able to carry Benjamin to the window and show him off to a friend. I was able to carry him without fear of setting off monitors or disturbing wires. But I had to be careful about how I walked, to not to trip over my gown or drop him.

This is the first time I have carried him and moved around. The other times I held him, he had been placed in my arms or I was already sitting down.

I felt so confident I could have run past the window — all the way outside. I felt confident enough to smile — to laugh.

I walked, I held him close, but as gently as I could. When I got to the window, I put him in the crook of my arm and tilted his head so that Jeff could see him. I had watched other dads hold their babies up with two hands, much like you would hold a puppy, with its legs dangling toward the floor. These dads were much more experienced and much more confident than I am, so I held Benjamin like a little girl would hold her favorite doll — except he was not a doll — he was alive and, yes, he does look like me.

When I got to the window, Jeff pecked on the glass, even though the only sign on the window says "Don't peck on the glass," and he laughed at Benjamin like adults do when they try to make the baby respond. Benjamin, probably for the first time in his life, was being carried around and showed off like babies are supposed to be. He acted like it was the most natural thing in the world — as if he were born to be admired — marveled over.

Nicki's mother Judy calls Benjamin a miracle baby. Before Benjamin became sick, I would have said that all babies are miracles, but now that's not true. In my life, in my heart, Benjamin is the only miracle baby that I know.

As I was showing him to my friend, family members of other babies gathered around and looked at Benjamin. Although I had never seen or met any of these people, and would probably never see them again, they shared the universal understanding that comes when a father shows off his son. I felt so proud.

I must have stayed at the window for several minutes before I suddenly became afraid that maybe I had been away too long. I hustled back toward Benjamin's crib, but when I got back, I realized that I could have stayed as long as I wanted. He was no longer tied to the monitors. He got his food from bottles, not tubes. There were no i.v.'s attached. He was as babies are supposed to be — free.

APRIL 26

DURING INFANT CPR CLASS, I broke the head off a dummy. Needless to say, the rest of the class was a disaster.

Now that we are in the process of getting ready to home, everything has accelerated to a rapid-fire pace. This morning I attended an infant CPR class — in case something ever happened to Benjamin. Of course, if that ever happens, there will need to be someone on hand to do adult CPR because I will need to be resuscitated as well.

A nurse named Lawson was my instructor. Although I didn't think the class was particularly informative, Nurse Lawson was a marvelous storyteller. When her children were still young, they had a pet skunk that had been descented. One day she came home and found out that the skunk had poisoned himself by eating a toadstool. Nurse Lawson reacted quickly by using the same poison control medicine used for babies — Ipecac — to save the skunk's life.

She also told me how CPR was created. Apparently, a group of doctors in Norway came up with the idea and had a dollmaker make the first dummy. When it came time to pick the face for the dummy, the dollmaker remembered a story that he had heard about a girl who had been found dead floating in the Seine River in Paris. Apparently, the girl's face was in all the newspapers throughout Europe, in an attempt to identify her. She was given the name Annie. Back then, the police would make a death mask of the person to use if they ever identified them. The dollmaker used this death mask as a model for the first dummy — thus the name of Resuscitating Annie.

The class was moving along at a wonderful pace until it came time for all of the participants to practice on the dummies that were provided. One of the first things that we had to do was gently pull the babies' heads back in order to clear the passageway. As I began to adjust my dummy, I snapped its head off, effectively killing the baby.

Not only were my efforts met with a great deal of laughter and a stern look from Nurse Lawson, but it further shook my already fragile confidence. I tried again and was so rattled that I messed up the steps. Nurse Lawson's patience was short, as you might expect from someone who had the presence of mind to give Ipecac to a sick skunk. After about an hour, I was finally able to get through the process. Somewhat reluctantly, Nurse Lawson signed off on my sheet saying that I was qualified to do infant CPR.

In actuality, I am not qualified to do infant CPR, but I am smart enough to know I do not possess the ability to save Benjamin's life. Therefore, if something bad happens, I will make sure I am around people such as Nicki and the grandparents who will be able to handle any sort of emergency that occurs.

Before our evening visit, Nicki and I went to the *Baby Superstore* to purchase what seemed like a million items, including a baby first aid kit. While there, I watched a mom and dad who had a toddler, probably between one and two years old because she was learning how to walk, travel through the isles. My attention was suddenly drawn to the family when the mother said, "Hey, aren't you watching the baby?" As I looked over at her, I saw that the baby girl had climbed up three steps of one of the big rolling ladders that was between the aisles to get items that were located on the upper shelves. Both parents looked more than competent. I was sufficiently panicked when I saw how quickly things go bad.

That situation was fresh in my mind when we arrived at the hospital for our evening visit. While Nicki was rocking Benjamin, and I was in my customary seat in the corner, I watched one of those horrible events that always seems to occur in slow motion — like when you see an animal hit by a car. The nurses were moving an isolette to make way for a new baby.

Unnoticed by the nurse doing the transfer, a monitor cord from the adjacent crib became snagged on the side of the isolette. As they were moving the isolette, the monitor was being pulled along the top shelf. I looked in horror as the monitor began to fall from the shelf, directly toward the baby underneath.

Like a lightening bolt, Nurse Carmen, who was stationed across the room, appeared from nowhere to put herself between the monitor and the baby. As the monitor fell, it struck Carmen on the shoulder and then fell harmlessly to the floor. Carmen did not have time to shout a warning. She just hurled herself over the baby and shielded him from danger much like a Secret Service agent is taught to protect the President. In the two months we had been in the nursery, it was the first time that I had seen this kind of near accident. I marveled at how quickly Carmen responded.

I suppose that part of being a parent is learning to deal with emergencies and the unexpected. It is difficult to plan for these things because you don't plan accidents — just how you will deal with them.

While all of this was going on, I caught a glimpse of Brandon, all by himself in the isolation room. Two new doctors had been brought in to evaluate him. Although no one is saying anything, it is apparent that he is not doing well. I overheard one of the nurses say that he had coded, which I think means his heart stopped, earlier that morning. There is a chance that he will not live through the day. I know the doctors and nurses will do what they can to save him, just like Carmen did when she threw herself over the baby. These people are trained to do anything at all to save a child. It is their first, best destiny. Sometimes, though, all of the training, all the skill in the world, can't make a difference.

Just as the couple we saw at the *Baby Superstore* did nothing wrong, their baby was two or three steps away from a tragedy, not because of a mistake, but just because sometimes terrible accidents happen. No matter how hard we try, or how prepared we are, there are certain things beyond our control.

APRIL 27

MONITOR CLASS WAS AWFUL. It took almost five hours. Nicki told me the instructor had a really annoying habit of saying, "My name is Donna. Are there any questions? This is a power cord. Are there any questions? You take the power cord and you plug it into the wall. Are there any questions?"

Nicki made the comment that if she were having any difficulty understanding the concept of plugging a power cord into the wall, then Benjamin's chances were absolute zero. Also, they did a test of the monitor. It let out a high-pitched screech that will send our dog into orbit. This monitor is five times louder than anything used at the hospital. If it does not wake Benjamin from an A&B spell, nothing will.

Early this morning, Nicki and I tried to assemble the stroller/car seat. We couldn't even find the instructions. After several hours, we decided to wait and call the store once it opened. When I got home from work to take Nicki to the hospital, I saw all the doors to her car standing open. I could see Nicki and Judy huddled in the backseat.

When I walked over, the two of them were complaining because it had taken over an hour for them to get the seat strapped in. They were both covered with perspiration from wrestling with the seatbelt. I was threatened with my life if I ever thought about removing that seat. The only positive is that Benjamin will be locked in so tightly that it will take a nuclear attack to dislodge him.

We are also stockpiling formula. The name of the formula Benjamin has been using at the hospital has been changed. The people at the *Baby Superstore* are trying to figure out which formula is the new one.

When we finally did get to the hospital, Benjamin did one of the sweetest things I have seen so far. As Nicki laid him up against her chest, he put his arms around her like he was trying to hug her. He also held his eyes open trying to watch her face. He is such a pleasant baby. He doesn't cry. He doesn't fuss. He just wants to cuddle and love. After being attached to all of the monitors for so long and being so sick, it is understandable. I am going to let him cuddle and love as much as he wants.

THE LONG WAY HOME

During the evening, I asked one of the nurses how Brandon was doing. She told me the concerns I had were real. There had been a long meeting the night before with the doctors. Apparently, they have run out of options. There is a lot of bleeding and they are doing transfusions just to keep him alive. He has coded twice. One time they thought they had lost him. This nurse told us that it was just a matter of waiting for him to die. I was so upset that I had to go outside. I walked around the building, even though it is misting rain. I needed to get away for awhile.

Brandon and Benjamin have spent so much time together in this nursery. His father and mother have been so friendly to us and supportive. One of the nurses told me that Brandon's mother was always upbeat about Brandon going home one day. She said his mom gets on the Internet every night looking for different things, different options, that might give them some hope — that might give Brandon a chance to live.

As I walked around the hospital, I let out a scream. I screamed really loud. It was a scream of frustration. A scream because a month ago this was Benjamin they were talking about. A scream because a month ago they were talking about Benjamin not living, not going home. A scream because there was nothing for me to do but scream. I don't know Brandon's parents well enough to say anything to them. Even if I did, I don't know what it would be. How do you tell someone you are sorry his or her child is dying — or is dead? I let out that scream because it's just not fair. Why this child? Why these people?

The scream was because I am ashamed. I am ashamed of the fact that I am glad that Benjamin is not the one dying — that Benjamin will go home. The scream was because there is something not right when a child dies. If babies die, they should die quickly. They shouldn't linger like Brandon has. They shouldn't have developed a personality. They shouldn't have become loved.

Brandon will never know a home other than the nursery. How much pain has this child endured? How much love has he felt? Is it worth it?

My scream was because this baby didn't die when he was born — because this baby is dying now. The scream was because I don't know what else to do but scream.

I walked faster. I wanted to run, but I can't. I wanted to get away somewhere. I don't know why this has hit me so hard, but it is smothering me. I feel the loss even though Brandon is not my child — even though I have not said much more than superficial words to his parents. I don't know where they are from. I don't know their story. I don't know how many other children they have. I don't know how they are taking all of this. I just know how it has affected me.

Why can't Brandon and Benjamin grow up together and be friends? They would be the same age. They could play ball together — go on double dates together. Now the only thing will be a tombstone with Brandon's birthday and death day on it. It is terrible that these two days are in the same year, so close together. Now every time I see a baby's tombstone, I will think it could have been for Benjamin. Brandon is the first baby I have

THE LONG WAY HOME

ever known that will die. As I think these thoughts, I become ashamed again because it means that I have given up hope. I remember back to the time when the doctors told us Benjamin might die that afternoon. Nicki would not let me give up hope. Yet, I have not learned my lesson because here I am walking around the hospital, yelling in the rain, and giving up hope for a boy I have never held or touched. I have never even taken a long look at him because we're not supposed to do this.

It's not right for me to give up hope. I don't have that right. It's not my call to make. It's for the parents and the doctors to give up hope — not me, a casual passerby — somebody who doesn't even know the family, or their names, to write this child off. I don't know what effect Brandon has had on the world or on people's lives, yet I will mourn his death.

If you truly believe that there is a purpose for all tragedy, then what can be the purpose of this? Am I even qualified to ask? Is it even fair for me to ask?

As I walk, I think and I fear. How long will this fear last? How long will I search for meaning? When will I not be unafraid? Am I going to feel this way every time someone dies?

I don't want to go back in the NICU because I don't want to see Brandon — not because of the suffering I feel for him, but because it makes me remember when Benjamin was so sick. But it is silly to stay out here and yell and it is selfish. So I walk. I will have to go back inside soon.

APRIL 28

BENJAMIN IS GOING HOME the day after tomorrow! He has been in the hospital for over two months and now we are finally going to take him home.

One of the traditions in the NICU is the selection of the outfit for the going-home photographs. Children's Hospital provides a photographer who takes going-home pictures of the babies and part of the process is the selection of the outfit for the pictures.

Nicki went through all of the clothes and ultimately picked a light green outfit with a cap that had pea pods printed on it. The whole atmosphere resembles graduation from high school. We spent the day getting Benjamin ready for his photograph and taking names and addresses from other families that we have gotten to know — and getting ourselves in the mind set to go home.

APRIL 29

THE CENTRAL POWER LINE that runs into our house blew a transformer, leaving us without electricity. The utility department came out and turned the power off until we could arrange for an electrician to come and put in new line. We were told that it would be three to four days before this could be done. Nicki broke down in tears.

She cried for a good part of the afternoon. She told me that she would probably die if she had to spend one more night in that hospital. This is the first time that she has really cried since all of this started. She openly wept for almost an hour. All I could do was hold my arms around her. She said she could not stand the thought of leaving Benjamin in the hospital for another night and that we had to find a way to bring him home.

Mom and Pop rose to the occasion. They went through the telephone book and found someone that would come out and do the work. Pop explained the problem to the electrician. When Nicki and I left to go to the hospital, Pop told me that he would see to it that the lights and air conditioning were back on by tomorrow morning.

We had a great lunch with Coulter's mom. Nicki presented her with a stuffed lamb. It was like the lamb in one of the SID's videos we saw during our parenting classes. This was one of the most horrifying videos I have ever seen. The video started with the lamb being placed in the crib next to the baby. When the parents stepped out of the room, the lamb came to life and announced to the audience that he was one of the things that kills your baby. He then explained about SIDs.

Toy stores sell a lamb that looks like the SID's lamb. I don't know why anyone would want a stuffed animal in the crib of his or her baby if it could be a killer, but for some reason, we thought that this would be a cool gift for Coulter!

In order to leave Children's Hospital, we had to spend the night with Benjamin in a room outside the NICU. Mom, Dad, and baby spend their first night alone together in a room on the second floor of Children's Hospital.

As we were saying our goodbyes, Dr. Prinz came over and gave me a long hug and told me that he was going to have to rethink his position on lawyers. He said Nicki and I would have to become a lot meaner or we would give lawyers a bad name. It was a kind gesture. It is sad to leave, but it is also a happy time.

We are running around doing all of the last-minute things that never seem to get done. Finally we were given a room assignment of 229 on the Second Floor. Lisa won the lottery and was given the honor of being our transport nurse. Even more fittingly, Coulter, who has been with Benjamin throughout the entire time, left about 45 minutes earlier.

As we walked through the door and out of the NICU to get onto the elevator, it was the first time that Benjamin has been out of the nursery and I am terribly scared. When we got to our room, I did my first unassisted feeding. Later, we turned on the television. The first time that Benjamin watched television, he saw *Thursday Night Thunder*, a professional wrestling program on cable. It is somewhat fitting.

As Nicki and I got ready for bed, we turned off the lights and realized that this is the first time that Benjamin has ever been in the dark. It is also the first time that it has ever been quiet. We wondered how he would react and constantly peeked over the side of the crib to see how he was doing. He was, of course, asleep.

Nicki lay on the bed provided for new mothers, while I was on the familiar Convert-A-Chair. We are so excited we are unable to sleep, knowing that if something went wrong, we are the only ones there to take care of Benjamin. Somehow we made it through the night.

Benjamin never cried. He never fussed. He just lay wrapped in his little blanket like he is supposed to. And just like parents are supposed to do, we held each other and hoped that we would be equal to the task.

APRIL 30

GOING HOME. This is the day we have been looking forward to for so long — a day that I honestly could not imagine two months ago — a day I am ready for.

This morning, Esther came by to see how Benjamin did last night. She was followed by several of the day nurses. I wish I had spent more time at the hospital during the mornings because Nicki's relationship with these nurses is wonderful. Esther and Nicki are like two good friends. I asked Esther if she was like this with all the families in the NICU. She said, "Nicki was easy to get attached to because of her endearing love for Benjamin and her interest in participating in his care." She also told me that because of Nicki, Benjamin had the best "buffed and shined" skin in the nursery! Esther also made me promise to make sure Pop got over his fear of holding Benjamin.

Dr. Buchheit came by a little before lunchtime to go over Ben's discharge summary. He spent almost an hour with us. He told us that everything looked great and told us about what to expect.

I thought back to the time when this man rattled me so badly — by telling me that Benjamin could die. He did his job that morning, just like he did his job for the next two months — which was to get to this day — a day when we could all go home. I asked Dr. Buchheit if he remembered scaring me so badly on that day we almost lost Benjamin. He did. He said what he remembered most, however, was how Nicki and I were never confrontational — that our understanding made his job so much easier. That floored me. I can't imagine anyone being anything but cooperative with the staff in the NICU. They give of themselves so completely. I always felt like we were on the same team.

Dr. Buchheit also told me I was the only person who ever sat on the floor outside his office reading the newspaper. He didn't know what to make of it at first, but once he realized that I was just there to get away from the NICU and was not trying to ambush him to ask questions, he thought it was kind of neat.

After Dr. Buchheit left, a steady stream of well-wishers from the NICU stopped by to pay their respects. Donna, the nurse that had been with Benjamin the day he almost died, came by because she wanted to hold him. The only time she was Benjamin's nurse was when he was so sick and could not be held. She said that she wanted to hold the miracle baby — the baby she had been rooting for these past two months.

Just before we left, Coby brought Coulter by and laid him on the bed next to Benjamin. It was amazing how still they both became when they looked at each other. Neither one of them had ever been this close to someone the same size before. They rolled their heads toward each other as their eyes went up and down, just looking at each other. They are so small.

I was sent to get the car. Nicki is bringing Benjamin, along with help from people from the hospital. I think to myself that on the way home, I will do the best driving of my life. This will become a constant theme. I will have to do everything better — be a better person, a better provider.

As Benjamin is wheeled outside, another in the long string of firsts occurs. This is the first time he has ever been outside. It is the first time that he has ever felt the sun, seen the sky, or smelled the air. Today is the first day for all of these things. It will be his first car ride. Everything is new. It will also be a day of firsts for me and for Nicki. It will be the first time I have ever driven a car with a baby as a passenger.

After Benjamin was placed securely in his car seat, the one that Nicki and Judy installed just a few days ago, I turned on the engine and pulled out. Somewhat appropriately, the Rolling Stones came on the radio, singing *You Can't Always Get What You Want*. As I pulled away from Children's Hospital, I realized there is something so true about this song — you don't always get what you want — but you do get what you need.

EPILOGUE

BY NICKI

LEAVING THE HOSPITAL was really only the beginning of Benjamin's success story. Since then he has continued to amaze us — and everyone who knows him — with his progress.

In May 1999, after two and a half months of being in the NICU, Dail and I brought our 8-pound baby boy Benjamin home. He was still on four different medicines, house quarantine, a heart monitor, and a special preemie formula that we could only find at one store. Dail and I joked that our baby was extra special because he came with a power cord.

At first, Benjamin wore the heart monitor all the time, but he improved so quickly that in a few weeks he only had to wear the monitor when he was sleeping. Being foolish and inexperienced new parents, we had been worried that we might not be able to hear the monitor's alarm. Those fears were immediately erased the first time the monitor went off in the middle of the night. When the alarm sounded, I jumped out of bed and ran to Benjamin's crib. I arrived in time to watch him wake up, take a deep breath, and then go back to sleep. I spent the rest of the night watching his chest rise and fall.

As stressful as those nights were, things did get better. By the end of the summer Benjamin was off all medicine, eating normal formula, and released from house quarantine. Home Health came every week to check the heart monitor, review the record of Benjamin's episodes, and make adjustments to the machine's settings. Suddenly, they told me they would be taking it away soon! The machine that had scared us so much when we left the hospital had become our safety net. Dail and I could sleep because we knew Benjamin was OK as long as he had the monitor strapped around his chest.

But our sense of security did not last long because one Thursday I was told Benjamin did not need monitoring any longer. The frequency and severity of his apnea episodes had decreased to the point that he was ready to come off the monitor. Now, that is not to say that the monitor never went off any more, because it still did, occasionally. On Friday, I tried to go without the monitor, but failed. Saturday Benjamin napped without it, but wore it throughout the night. Sunday was the same. Monday they picked up the machine. Monday night I watched him breathe.

But again, things got better. We learned to live, and sleep, without the monitor. By this time therapy had started. First

EPILOGUE

there was occupational therapy for Benjamin's left arm and hand. PVL had left Benjamin with a mild form of cerebral palsy that manifested itself in decreased movement in his left arm and a clenched left fist. He was fitted for the first of many hand braces designed to make his left hand stay open. We worked on trying to get him to play with objects with his left hand with little success. Benjamin had little awareness of any part of the world that was on his left side. Dail and I did things like approach him from the left, talk to him from his left, and hold him so that someone would be on his left side — anything to make him look to his left.

We also tried weight bearing with his left arm with little success because the strength he had in his arm was poor. It was as if his arm were asleep. When we tried to make him use it, he probably had a bad sensation — like when we get "pins and needles." So we focused elsewhere for the time being.

Robyn, his therapist, taught Benjamin to roll from his back over onto his belly. This was a huge step for Benjamin. Next, we worked on sitting up, but found that Benjamin lacked strength in his trunk muscles. So his doctor added water therapy to his weekly schedule. Benjamin and I, and our therapist, would all hop in the pool and work on strengthening his trunk. He soon mastered splashing. Before long we saw great results and Benjamin could hold himself up in a seated position. He continued water therapy until a long run of ear infections caused us to give up the pool.

Next we returned to weight bearing with his left arm, hoping it would lead to crawling. It did not. Benjamin never crawled. To this day, crawling has never been Benjamin's chosen form of movement. He would just roll across the floor to where he wanted to go and then sit up. Go with what you know, I guess!

After Benjamin mastered the roll-and-sit, we began speech therapy — not for talking — but because it was time to move on to solid foods and Benjamin had a bad case of texture aversion. He didn't like to even touch food much less have someone put it in his mouth. This problem was quickly overcome, and Benjamin became a member of the Big Eater's Club. Now speech therapy would be about getting Benjamin to talk more.

Physical therapy was our next big hurdle. It was time to work on leg strength and get this boy up and walking. To facilitate the process, Benjamin was fitted with his first set of leg braces. We entered him in a program during the winter called Children's Corner where he would go for therapy three days a week, all day long. The program allowed him to have three hours of therapy each day — OT, PT, and speech — and lunch and a nap, as well as participation in group activities. This was a period of intensive therapy for Benjamin that he did not always like. Benjamin fell so much when he was learning to walk that he wore a soft foam "crash" helmet all the time. We got the helmet after a trip to the emergency room because Benjamin fell and got a concussion. But, still, he was making remarkable progress. Falling was just a part of it. I don't think Dail and I respond like normal parents anymore — Benjamin is going to fall and he has to learn to pick himself up. Dail started calling him "Crash Bandicott."

EPILOGUE

In January 2000, just before his first birthday, Benjamin started to have seizures —not even "normal" seizures, if there is such a thing. Benjamin was having something called "infantile spasms." In plain language that just meant bad news. Infantile spasms result in more brain damage and regression. Now he was faced with the possibility of losing all the skills we had worked so hard to develop in the past year. Benjamin had gotten to the point were he was interactive with the people around him. He would smile and laugh all the time he and was really just a joy. Now we were facing the possibility of having to watch the gleam in his eyes fade away.

Benjamin was admitted to Children's Hospital so that a 24-hour EEG and an MRI could be performed. To have the EEG, Benjamin had 25 or so electrodes glued to his head. Then all the cords were wrapped up under bandages that looked like a turban. Next, he was attached to the machine and put in his room in front of a video camera. The physicians wanted to be able to watch the seizures, too. So here we were — all us confined to a room. Benjamin looked like a little wounded soldier. It was a terrible day.

Robert and Coby were in a room on the same floor because Coulter had to have emergency surgery on his shunt and had been checked in the same day as Benjamin. We decided that the boys must have called ahead to be sure that other one was going to be at the hospital so they could be there at the same time.

Benjamin had the MRI the next night at Fort Sanders Hospital which is adjacent to Children's Hospital. He saw his first snow that night as we walked between the two buildings.

After he was released from the hospital, Benjamin never had another infantile spasm. The seizure episode had lasted 14 days — spontaneous remission is what they told us. This is not a common occurrence at all. I decided that Benjamin must have hated his stay in the hospital so much that he decided that was enough. This particular type of seizure is not likely to recur, but Benjamin still remains at high risk to develop a seizure disorder, so every six months we go for a check-up with his neurologist.

With the seizure crisis over, Benjamin returned to therapy and it was business as usual. His first birthday passed with a feeling of relief, knowing we had just dodged a major bullet.

Now, at age two, Benjamin is an example of a modern-day miracle. Every day he achieves things that two years ago we never thought would be possible. When Benjamin was in the NICU, he was so sick I could not even hold him. Now he moves so fast, I cannot catch him.

Benjamin has been released from Children's Corner and receives OT and PT as an outpatient. He participates in a language group to get him to talk more. His vocabulary consists of only a few words so far: bear, pear, go, car, bye, cow, kitty, and pig. He loves the language group and every day or so he looks at us and out comes a new word. Just today while Dail was in the bathroom, Benjamin said "pee." My only comment was "at least he is talking."

EPILOGUE

Benjamin has gone through two sets of leg braces and recently graduated to using only hard plastic shoe inserts. He has mastered walking and is working on running and climbing stairs. He no longer uses the "crash" helmet, although we are thinking about kneepads at this point! Benjamin has been through more hand braces than I can count and he will continue to wear one for a long time. He is starting to use his left arm a lot now, but he still has difficulty with grasp and release in his left hand. But we knew from the start that we would be working on this for a long time.

Benjamin developed a "lazy eye" earlier this year and has been wearing a patch over his strong eye for the last two months or so. To us this is no big deal compared to everything else he has been through. I still get questions all the time when I go to the grocery store, such as "What's wrong with your baby." But I just think to myself — nothing — he is a miracle baby.

Benjamin and Coulter are still big buddies and have regular play dates together. Two of Benjamin godparents, Jenny and Jeff, started dating and have gotten married. Benjamin was in the wedding because their first date came as a result of a late-night run to the drugstore for medicine. We didn't know it at the time, but Benjamin was a little matchmaker.

As for Dail and me, well, I guess we are still recovering emotionally from the whole ordeal. The time in the hospital before Benjamin was born, and afterward in the NICU, took a heavy toll on both of us. Dail wrote this book and I — well — I just cry every time I read it. We have recently started to talk about the possibility of having more children and I find that it brings all the emotions back to the surface again. The chance of another pre-term delivery scares me to death. With Benjamin, my pregnancy was high-risk to start with and for another pregnancy I would be even more so. I will have to see if I can find the strength within myself to face this again.

When I look back and remember all the things that have happened to Benjamin, I am just so thankful that we came through it and have this wonderful baby boy with us and that he won't remember any of this. One day when he is older, I will tell him the story of how he entered this world. I will show him the old photographs and explain to him how he got the scars on his arms and head.

Scars heal, and some memories fade, but Dail and I will always remember. Each night, after I rock him to sleep, I carry Benjamin to his bed. He has a little baby pillow that was mine when I was a baby. As I lay his head against the softness of that pillow, he looks like an angel. And it is then when I realize that Benjamin and I must have had a pretty special angel watching over us.

I love him so much.

EPILOGUE

Someday I Am Going to Thank You

My father held me twice before I got sick.
It happened quick —
      like an eye-blink.
When you wouldn't let my mother pick me up
You placed her hand upon my chest
So that she could feel it rise and fall
      like the slow break of waves across a beach at nighttime.
I don't know what you did
      or why you did it
But it made me well.
Sometimes it hurt,
      but I don't remember being scared.
Sometimes it felt like I should sleep
      but it never got dark.

While I was here
Babies came
    and went.
Some stopped being babies and became angels.
Their beds were always filled
    and tomorrow always came.
Even with the beeps
    and the talking
You could always feel the quiet when a parent cried.

I have no memory of faces
    or words.
I didn't even know what words were.
The sounds mixed together like spilled colors.
What I remember is your touch.

Because of you
I am me.
Because of you
My father
    and my mother
And their fathers
    and their mothers
Survived the long walks away from my bed.
Because of you
I will one day have the chance to help someone like me.

EQUAL TO THE TASK

On that day
  in the stillness of a private moment
Without words
I will thank you.

Benjamin Dail Cantrell
February 25, 2000

PUBLISHER'S NOTE: Dail Cantrell wrote this poem as a tribute to the nurses in the Neonatal Intensive Care Unit at Children's Hospital in Knoxville, Tennessee. He presented a framed copy of the poem to the nurses on Benjamin's first birthday. The poem now hangs in the NICU.